## *Praise for* Conscious Creation

"*Conscious Creation* is a powerful call to reflect on the inner state from which leadership emerges. Nader Vasseghi provides a clear path for bridging the gap between intention and impact. This book elevates leaders beyond performance and into a state of presence, where responsibility and integrity shape every decision. If leadership is creation, this is a guide to creating wisely."

**Merrick Rosenberg**, Founder and CEO of Take Flight Learning, author of *Personality Intelligence* and *The Chameleon*

"Conscious Creation is a rare leadership book: deeply lived, globally relevant, and genuinely useful for founders, executives, and investors building in an AIdriven world. It's a book to practice, not just to read."

**Kamran Elahian**, High-Tech Entrepreneur with 4 unicorn IPO's

"As a business leader who's been striving to rescue a 30-year-old family business from existential crisis, this book found me at the perfect time. I can set ambitious goals for the oversea deep-tech companies our company acquired recently, but Nader reminds me that "*goals live in the future, while intentions live in the present. Intentions can be renewed before a conversation, a meeting, or a difficult decision*". There are so many other similar subtle wisdoms shared in this book, wisdoms that will impact the long-term outcomes if you internalize and practice them in your daily life. I wholeheartedly recommend this book."

**Justin Wang**, Radiant Opto-Electronics Chairman and President

"In *Conscious Creation,* Nader Vasseghi provides an essential framework for the modern leader. Strategic brilliance alone is insufficient —real impact is defined by the consciousness from which we lead. Vasseghi moves beyond traditional command-and-control models to explore the foundational pillars of leadership: presence, attunement, and intention. This book is a vital guide for any executive looking to cultivate the high-level psychological safety and collective intelligence necessary to lead teams through the complexity of the AI era. It is deeply insightful and timely."

**Andrew Dahlkemper** has served as a Human Resources leader for global, multibillion-dollar companies, including Google, Dolby Labs, and Electronic Arts.

"*Conscious Creation* reframes leadership at its core. It moves beyond strategy and execution to what truly drives outcomes—the leader's inner state and its impact on others. After working with Nader for years, I've seen firsthand how transformative this perspective is. This is essential reading for leaders operating in today's complex, high-stakes world."

**Sobhan Khani**, President and Partner at Plug and Play Ventures

"Nader Vasseghi has challenged me to examine the inner state from which I lead and live. Conscious Creation reframes leadership as something purposeful—shaping joy, impact, and an abundant life for ourselves and those we touch. That shift eases the quiet angst of a results-only mindset and replaces it with clarity that feels genuinely liberating."

**Brad Mountz**, President at Mountz Inc.

"*Conscious Creation* challenged me to think differently about leadership. Truly compelling from start to finish, it kept me engaged throughout. It served as a mirror—highlighting my strengths while illuminating the gaps in my own leadership, expanding my perspective without requiring me to change my unique style. Every chapter contributes to a deeper awakening, making it a meaningful read for anyone committed to growth and intentional leadership."

**Kiran Rupal**, DDS president & owner

# Conscious Creation

# Conscious Creation

## LEADERSHIP
## AT THE SOURCE
## OF THE FUTURE

**Nader Vasseghi**

Published by Cnergist

ISBN (paperback): 979-8-9967536-0-4
ISBN (ebook): 979-8-9967536-1-1

Book design and production by www.AuthorSuccess.com

Printed in the United States of America

## Dedication

To my parents,
whose love and support continue to guide me.

To Firozeh,
for sharing this journey with me.

To my children—Nima, Navid, and Omid—
for all that you have taught me, often in ways I did not expect.

And to the many leaders I have had the privilege to work with,
whose courage and openness continue to shape and deepen this path.

# Contents

# Foreword

A large portion of my career as a coach and seminar leader was spent working with corporate and non-profit leaders and managers. To give my work depth, I spent countless hours reading books on leadership, hoping I was never missing anything new or innovative in the field.

However, as good as many of those books were, there was always something missing in each one of them. Some over-compensated on the spiritual and psychological side, leaving out practical, tough-minded, real-world execution. Others stressed the tactics and systems involved in managing employees toward higher performance and productivity, without addressing the leader's inner world.

So it took a lot of reading for me to learn the whole picture of what a thoroughly effective leader looked like. I combined that reading with seminars I took and, most importantly, with my own experience working with leaders.

Now it amazes me and somewhat amuses me to read and then re-read this rather startling book by Nader Vasseghi!

It amazes me because for the first time in the history of books on this subject, his prescription for powerful leadership is whole and complete. It gives you the whole powerful algorithm with absolutely nothing left out.

It amuses me to think of how much of my time would have been saved if I had possessed this book to begin with and used it as my conceptual guideline for all my teaching and coaching. But that's just a fantasy because the time would not have been right for this book back then. The world wasn't ready for it.

To those of you starting a career right now of leadership or leadership coaching this is truly the only book you will ever need.

It strikes, with great poetic force, every cylinder.

Perhaps only Nader Vesseghi could have written this book. Aside from being a proven and sought-after leadership coach and consultant, he is also an entrepreneur and a gifted and creative musician. You'll get that heady feeling while reading this book that it is not the work of a mere cold-blooded businessman. There is renaissance in these eloquent pages.

And courage. What other thought leader in the world of business would have included a section on "Conscious breath" as being a vital part of the inner work and self-mastery that is the vital first stage of becoming a great leader?

The first part of the book could have been a book in itself, not because of length or because you find all the powerful points made in this book to be short and sweet, but because it is so thorough in giving the full spectrum of psychological and spiritual needs for a leader to do their work, coming from authenticity, integrity, and inner peace.

Part two is about "Leading with others." And right there, even in the title of the section, you realize that this work is not like other leadership approaches. Notice that Vasseghi does not call it "Leading others." That's because old-school hierarchical leadership approaches based on persuasion and manipulation by a superior to a subordinate are not in play. This section is inspired and enlightened in the way it guides us out of trying to lead others and moves us into the far more effective and collaborative domain in which we lead with others.

Just how do we do that? You'll be surprised with how convincingly the author walks you through the four practices of "Conscious Listening, Conscious Relating, Conscious Loving, and Conscious Coaching." Many books suggest that leaders do more listening, but that's as far as they go. This book goes all the way, and it's bold and beautiful. This is the courage to be thorough.

After the first two parts of this book, I was totally hooked on how revolutionary and valuable this book is. I already couldn't wait to get it into the hands of leaders and coaches of leaders I know who will appreciate me beyond belief for giving them this guide to the future of great leadership.

I certainly wasn't expecting Part Three to take me to a whole new level of excitement. I mean, after the surprising section on "conscious loving" as an effective leadership activity, how much higher could this go?

But the third part absolutely rockets beyond the launch pads of parts one and two.

This is the part that, in Vasseghi's words, "turns leadership outward—toward impact and responsibility. Here, leadership is measured by what it sets in motion and what it leaves behind. We explore how leaders relate to the weight of their actions as creators of futures, cultures, and conditions for life."

Ah, yes, this is the part that the skeptics were waiting for. The part that some readers might have worried might even be absent, given the loving mindfulness, relationship, and inner awareness prescribed in parts one and two.

This is the action part. This is where the impact of conscious leadership is nurtured and delivered. This is where the secret behind Nader Vasseghi's successful track record coaching leaders and whole companies is revealed. This is how his clients transform.

In his words, "Transformation is often misunderstood as improvement—becoming more skilled, more efficient, or more capable within an existing identity. But conscious transformation is something else entirely. It is not an upgrade to the current self. It is a crossing of a threshold."

Yes! That's exactly what this book was for me. The crossing of a threshold from who I used to be as a coach of leaders and leadership coaches, to who I am now, with the guidance of this book.

He writes, "At moments of true transformation, what is required is not addition, but release. Old identities loosen. Familiar ways of knowing lose their authority. The strategies that once brought success no longer produce coherence. What worked before begins to constrain what wants to emerge next."

I'll save how he stands and delivers the transformation for real-world action and impact in part three for your own enjoyment and excitement. You will not be disappointed.

For now, I'll just stand by my response to Nader after first reading this book in manuscript: "I can hear the harmonic sounds of the multiverse celebrating this rich and abundant book that takes leadership in a thrilling ride into a level of consciousness not yet attained by any author. Lucid, practical, thorough . . . deeply and permanently inspiring!!!"

Steve Chandler
Scottsdale, Arizona
February 2026

# Introduction

It was about two years into the start-up I had founded. We were no longer in the honeymoon phase. We were in the proving phase. The company was young. The economy was unstable. Cash mattered. Momentum mattered. Every quarter mattered.

Six of us sat around the conference table reviewing the sales pipeline. The numbers were clear: we were behind our targets. Deals were slipping.

My head of sales methodically walked us through the pipeline. The gap was undeniable.

Inside me, urgency rose.

As CEO, I felt responsible for protecting the company's future. This was not the moment to ease up. It was the moment to raise the standard, question assumptions, and sharpen strategy.

I leaned forward.

My questions grew sharper. My tone more intense. I pressed on the weak spots in the plan. I challenged the thinking. In my mind, I was helping. I was rallying the team.

Then I saw it.

Tears gathering in her eyes.

She stood up abruptly and walked out of the room.

Silence followed her. No one spoke.

I sat there, confused and unsettled, aware that something had just shifted.

I ended the meeting and followed her into the parking lot.

"What just happened?" I asked.

She turned toward me, shaken.

"You shouted at me," she said. "I'm giving this everything I have, and you blame me. Right now, I feel like a failure."

Her words landed harder than any missed revenue target.

Whether I had shouted or not no longer mattered. In her experience, I had.

The irony was painful. I respected her deeply. I admired her ownership and discipline. I trusted her fully.

Yet what I intended as urgency landed as blame.

What I believed was leadership felt overwhelming.

What I thought was rallying felt like an attack.

In that moment, I encountered something I had never fully seen before:

The gap between intention and impact.

Over the next several days, the incident stayed with me. I replayed it. Reflected on it. Sat with the discomfort of realizing that my presence had transmitted something I did not consciously intend.

That was the beginning.

The beginning of understanding that leadership is more than strategy and execution.

It is transmission.

It shapes the emotional climate of a room.

It shapes how people see themselves.

It shapes what expands, and what quietly contracts.

Leadership is always creating something. The question is whether we are conscious of what we are creating.

This book was born from that rupture.

In the days that followed, I began to question something deeper than my tone in a meeting; I began to question my understanding of leadership itself.

I had believed leadership was defined by clarity of vision, strength of will, and force of execution. I believed that if my intention was good and my strategy sound, the rest would follow.

I was wrong.

Leadership is not defined merely by skill, intention, or strategic brilliance. It is defined by what we bring into being in people, in culture, and in the futures we quietly set in motion.

What moved through me in that room was not malicious. It was urgency. Pressure. Responsibility. But unexamined urgency does not stay contained within the leader. It transmits. It shapes emotional climate. It shapes identity. It shapes what contracts and what expands.

That realization changed the trajectory of my leadership and my understanding of it.

That moment in the parking lot marked the beginning of a deeper inquiry. Over the past two decades, as a founder, executive coach, and advisor to CEOs and leadership teams across industries, I have seen this same pattern repeat: high-performing leaders with strong intention creating unintended consequences. The work that emerged from that rupture became the foundation of my leadership practice and the framework you are about to explore.

Today, leaders operate in a world where technology and artificial intelligence amplify decisions at unprecedented speed and reach. What once affected a small team now shapes organizations, markets, and societies. What once dissipated over time now embeds itself into systems.

In such a world, leadership is no longer only about outcomes. It is about the consciousness from which those outcomes are created.

## What Makes Leadership Conscious?

At its core, consciousness is about being awake and aware. Conscious leadership begins with recognizing that every decision arises from an inner state—from assumptions, fears, values, beliefs, intentions, and unexamined patterns.

To lead consciously is to bring awareness to three essential dimensions:

- ✦ **Awareness of Self:** understanding the inner forces that shape perception, reaction, and motivation.
- ✦ **Awareness of Others:** recognizing that leadership is relational and that presence affects how others experience themselves.
- ✦ **Awareness of Impact:** seeing beyond immediate outcomes to the longer-term consequences embedded in culture, systems, and future conditions.

Conscious leadership does not reject ambition, execution, or effectiveness. It deepens them. It asks not only *what are we achieving,* but *what are we reinforcing as we achieve it?*

Effectiveness alone is not enough. History offers powerful examples of leaders who were extraordinarily effective and whose impact shaped humanity in profoundly different ways. Leadership is creation. And creation carries responsibility.

Leadership begins wherever choice, influence, and responsibility are present in our lives. It is not reserved for titles or positions. It unfolds in families, teams, organizations, and communities. In how we speak. In how we decide. In what we allow and what we challenge.

Every act of leadership shapes something beyond ourselves, often more than we realize.

In the modern era, where technology and artificial intelligence give leaders exponential reach, the consequences of leadership decisions are profoundly amplified. A single choice can shape cultures, markets, and futures at unprecedented scale. When those choices arise from fear, ego, or narrow self-interest, the damage is no longer local or temporary; it becomes systemic and enduring.

This is why conscious leadership is no longer a preference or a style. It is an imperative.

## Why Now?

We are at a tipping point. The exponential growth of technology, the accelerating impact of climate change, and widening social and political unrest all point to one thing: the old models of leadership are no longer sufficient.

Traditional leadership has often emphasized control, efficiency, and short-term results. But in today's volatile, uncertain, and complex world, we need leaders who can navigate ambiguity, adapt wisely, and think holistically. We need leaders who are not focused solely on personal or organizational success, but on the well-being of humanity and the planet.

As leaders, we are called to be more than just effective. We are called to be conscious creators of beauty, strength, and love in ourselves, in others, and out in the world.

The future of our organizations, our communities, and our planet depends on it.

## What to Expect in This Book

In the chapters ahead, we will explore how conscious leadership unfolds in three interconnected dimensions: self-mastery, relational leadership, and creating long-term impact. Each section is designed to help you deepen your awareness, grow your leadership capacity, and make a meaningful impact.

### Part One: Leading from Within

The journey starts within. Before leadership shows up in decisions, relationships, or systems, it takes shape inside you. The inner state from which you lead—your intention, regulation, posture, and capacity for awareness—quietly determines the quality of everything that follows. This is the domain of self-mastery.

This first part focuses on four foundational capacities of inner leadership. We begin with Conscious Intention, clarifying the deeper source from which your leadership arises. Conscious Breath restores choice at the most fundamental level, grounding leadership in presence rather than reactivity. Conscious Stance examines the inner posture from which you meet pressure, uncertainty, and responsibility. Finally, Conscious Cultivation turns inner leadership into an ongoing practice. Specifically, how you tend your inner world so your highest self can be brought into the world.

### Part Two: Leading with Others

Leadership comes alive in a relationship. Every decision, every conversation, every moment of tension or trust unfolds between people. How you listen, respond, and relate shapes not only outcomes, but the quality of connection and ownership that emerges around you. This is the terrain of relational leadership.

In this part, we explore how leadership becomes a lived relationship rather than a role. We begin with Conscious Listening, where leaders learn to receive others without judgment and connect at a deeper level. Conscious Relating examines how leaders meet difference, tension, and conflict without collapsing into reactivity or control. Conscious Loving explores love not as sentiment, but as a leadership capacity embracing humanity without judgment and inviting others to unfold into their best. Finally, Conscious Coaching focuses on how leaders support growth and accountability without rescuing, fixing, or diminishing others' agency.

### Part Three: Leading with Impact

Part Three turns leadership outward toward impact and responsibility. Here, leadership is measured by what it sets in motion and what it leaves behind.

We begin with Conscious Choice, where leaders learn to choose from awareness rather than impulse, thus claiming authorship at the source of action. Conscious Creation deepens this responsibility, examining the impact of what leaders bring into the world through their decisions, structures, and systems. Conscious

Healing addresses how leaders restore wholeness, coherence, and flow within themselves, relationships, and organizations. Conscious Transformation marks the passage where leadership is no longer something you do, but something you become through the release of what no longer fits and the emergence of what must come next.

Each part of this book combines insight with practice. Alongside the conceptual frameworks, you will find reflections and practical exercises designed to help you embody conscious leadership, not merely understand it.

This book will strengthen your capacity to lead with clarity, composure, and conscious impact in a world of increasing complexity and scale. You will:

- ✦ Cultivate inner mastery by learning to regulate pressure, clarify intention, and lead from awareness rather than reaction.
- ✦ Elevate your relational leadership by building trust, ownership, and accountability through conscious listening, presence, and courageous dialogue.
- ✦ Expand your impact by making choices and designing systems that create long-term value beyond short-term wins.

This book is an invitation to lead as a conscious creator; to recognize that leadership is already unfolding through you in moments of choice, in how you meet pressure, and in what you reinforce or reshape.

The future is being shaped now through the consciousness from which you lead.

# PART I

# Leading From Within

CHAPTER 1

# Conscious Intention

*In the universe, there is an immeasurable, indescribable force which shamans call intent, and absolutely everything that exists in the entire cosmos is attached to intent by a connecting link.*

—Carlos Castaneda

Every act of creation begins with intention. Before every word spoken, every decision made, and every action taken, there is an invisible source—a quiet intent that shapes what follows. Most of the time, what moves us operates below the level of awareness, guided by habit, conditioning, fear, or the need for control. But when intention is brought into awareness, it shifts from an unconscious drive into a conscious act of creation. This is where conscious leadership begins.

Leadership is often described in terms of vision, strategy, execution, and results. Yet beneath all of these lies a more fundamental question: *From what inner source is this leadership arising?* Two leaders can pursue the same goal, apply the same strategy, and make similar decisions—yet create radically different outcomes in trust, culture, and long-term impact. The difference is not only *what* they do, but the consciousness from which they act.

Conscious intention is the alignment between who we are and what we do. It is the moment when action begins to reflect essence—the deeper intelligence, creativity, and values that live within us. When intention flows from this alignment, leadership carries coherence. Decisions feel grounded. Relationships deepen. Action moves with clarity rather than force. Leadership becomes less about pushing outcomes and more about allowing something true to take form.

Most people set goals. Few consistently lead from intention. Goals organize effort toward external aims. Intention emerges from inner vision—an expression of essence seeking form.

Goals are shaped by the mind and oriented toward achievement. Intention arises from being and expresses what we choose to embody. Goals focus on outcomes; intention shapes the energy, integrity, and consciousness we bring to the path itself.

Conscious leaders understand this distinction. They recognize that the energy behind an action is as consequential as the action itself. When intention is clear and aligned, even ordinary actions generate trust and meaning. When intention is distorted—by ego, fear, or the need to prove—even well-intended goals can create pressure, confusion, and unintended harm.

To live with conscious intention is to return, again and again, to essence—the place where contribution feels natural rather than forced. It is the zone where doing becomes an expression of being, and effort gives way to alignment. In that space, purpose is no longer something to chase or manufacture; it is something remembered.

Purpose, in this sense, is not a slogan or a strategy. It is the natural direction of our being when we are present, grounded, and connected. It is an inner compass that quietly guides us toward contribution and coherence. When leaders operate from this place, intention is no longer a mental exercise—it becomes a lived orientation.

Before systems, strategies, or skills, there is awareness of the energy from which we act. The quality of that energy shapes the reality we create.

To lead consciously is to live intentionally: to act from the inside out, aligning each choice with essence and purpose. When intention is clear, impact becomes coherent. When being and doing are aligned, leadership becomes not just effective, but artful.

## The Silent Architect of Reality

Before every visible creation, there is an invisible preparation.

Just as a building begins with a blueprint and music emerges from silence, every result we experience in life and leadership begins with intention.

Intention is the silent architect of reality—the unseen pattern that shapes form and outcome. We may not always recognize it, but the energy with which we approach anything determines the quality of what unfolds.

Two leaders can deliver the same message, implement the same strategy, or pursue the same goal; yet one creates trust, inspiration, and alignment, while the other breeds resistance and fear. The difference is not in what they do, but in the energy behind it, their underlying intention.

"Form follows frequency."

As a metaphor, this reminds us that outer results often reflect inner states. The quality of our thinking, emotion, and intention shapes the way our actions are received and the environments we create.

When our intention is pure and aligned with truth, the outcome reflects coherence, integrity, and flow. When our intention is clouded by ego, fear, or control, the outcome carries that distortion, no matter how polished the strategy.

As leaders, this is easy to overlook. We often focus on doing—on achieving goals, fixing problems, and driving results. But conscious leadership begins by asking a subtler question:

*What energy is moving through me as I act?*

The conscious leader recognizes that the outer world is a mirror of inner alignment. If there is conflict, miscommunication, or stagnation around them, it often points to an unexamined intention within them.

This awareness is humbling and empowering. It invites us to take full responsibility, not just for our actions, but for the consciousness from which those actions arise.

In this sense, leadership is not about control, but about coherence. We don't force outcomes; we attune to the frequency that allows them to unfold naturally. When we act from a state of clarity, trust, and service, we create harmony around us. When we act from tension, fear, or self-importance, we unknowingly spread that same vibration into the field of our teams and organizations.

The more conscious we become of our intentions, the more deliberate we become in shaping reality. Awareness turns leadership from reaction to creation—from managing circumstances to shaping the inner conditions from which outcomes arise.

And when intention and awareness align, our presence itself begins to lead; silently, powerfully, and effortlessly.

## The Hidden Forces That Shape Intention

Every intention carries energy—yet not all of it is conscious.

Beneath our words and actions lie subtle motivations that influence what we create. We may believe we are acting from clarity, but often our intentions are shaped by unexamined patterns: the desire to be right, to be liked, to be in control, or to be seen as good.

These hidden forces are the quiet architects of misalignment. They masquerade as purpose but are fueled by fear. A leader may intend to "empower others" but unconsciously seek validation. Another may intend to "drive excellence" but be motivated by the fear of being perceived as weak. On the surface, the intentions seem noble; beneath, they are reactive.

These are what I call the **compensatory acts of the ego**—attempts to fill an inner void by controlling outer circumstances. The ego, by nature, seeks to protect and defend. It wants certainty, security, and recognition. Yet in doing so, it subtly distorts our intention from creation to compensation.

Unconscious intention is like tinted glass: it colors everything we see and do without our awareness. It doesn't mean our goals are wrong; it simply means the energy behind them is mixed.

The first step toward conscious intention is not to fix these patterns but to **see** them. Awareness itself is the purifier. When we notice the fear beneath the ambition, the need for approval beneath the generosity, something shifts. The light of awareness dissolves distortion.

This is why self-observation is the foundation of leadership presence. It invites us to pause and look within before acting, to ask, *What is truly moving me right now?*

When the answer is rooted in fear, the energy feels tight and effortful. When it's rooted in essence, it feels open and alive. The body knows the difference even when the mind rationalizes.

A conscious leader learns to sense this difference—not as judgment, but as information. They recognize when their energy contracts, signaling the ego's grip, and when it expands, signaling alignment with truth. Awareness doesn't eliminate the ego; it integrates it.

By acknowledging our reactive motives with honesty and compassion, we free the energy trapped in them. That energy becomes available for creation instead of defense.

The journey from unconscious to conscious intention is not about perfection. It's about presence. Each time we become aware of what drives us, we step closer to alignment. Each moment of awareness refines the energy behind our actions.

When we purify intention through awareness, our leadership becomes lighter—not because there are fewer challenges, but because we no longer carry the weight of pretense. Our doing emerges from being, not from effort or striving.

One of the most common sources of confusion arises when intention is mistaken for desire.

## Intention Versus Desire

At first glance, intention and desire can appear similar. Both involve wanting, both move us toward action, and both shape our reality. Yet their origins—and their impact—are profoundly different.

**Desire** arises from a sense of lack. It says, *I don't have something, and I must get it in order to be happy.*

**Intention** arises from a sense of wholeness. It says, *I am aligned with my essence, and I choose to express from it.*

Desire is fueled by wanting to acquire, achieve, or prove. It's often tied to egoic identity—to who we think we should be or what we believe we need to feel complete. It chases fulfillment in the external world. And even when it succeeds, the satisfaction fades quickly, replaced by the next pursuit.

Intention, on the other hand, originates from being. It expresses the natural movement of our essence—the quiet impulse of creation that flows when we are connected to ourselves. It doesn't chase; it allows. It doesn't seek to possess; it seeks to express.

Desire is like wind on the surface of the ocean—restless, reactive, and easily swayed by circumstance.

Intention is the current beneath—steady, unseen, and powerful enough to shape the tide.

When we act from desire, we often find ourselves exhausted, striving, and dissatisfied, even when we achieve what we wanted. When we act from intention, we experience clarity, flow, and meaning, even in the face of challenge.

In leadership, this difference is profound. A leader driven by desire becomes attached to outcomes—market share, recognition, and results. A leader guided by intention focuses on alignment—clarity of purpose, integrity of process, and energetic coherence. The results still come, but they are byproducts of coherence rather than conquest.

Desire contracts awareness to the self; intention expands it to include others.

Desire grasps for control; intention collaborates with life.

Desire seeks success to satisfy the ego; intention seeks to serve beyond the self.

This is not to condemn desire—it has its place as a spark of movement. But when left unchecked, it becomes the fuel of ego and anxiety. When integrated into conscious intention, it transforms into vitality, an energy directed by awareness rather than craving.

To recognize the difference, we can simply pause before acting and ask:

*Is this coming from fear or from fullness? From craving or from allowing?*

When the movement arises from fullness—from alignment with essence and purpose—there is peace even in effort. When it arises from lack, there is tension even in success.

True intention is not about getting something. It's about giving expression to what wants to unfold within us.

It's not a grasping outward, but an unfolding inward—a movement from the essence of who we are into the world of what we create.

Michael was a respected executive known for his confidence and polished leadership style. His company had grown quickly, but something beneath the surface was faltering. Morale was low. Teams operated in silos. Communication had become cautious, and innovation had slowed to a trickle.

Determined to "empower others," Michael launched an initiative to decentralize decision-making and give his leaders more autonomy.

On paper, it looked progressive. In meetings and town halls, he spoke passionately about trust and collaboration. He emphasized ownership and encouraged people to step up. Yet despite the language of empowerment, little actually changed. Managers hesitated to make bold decisions, waiting for Michael's approval. Team members continued to look to him for direction. The structure had shifted, but the energy had not.

During a coaching session, I asked him a simple question.

"Why do you want to empower your team?"

Michael answered without hesitation, "Because I believe in them. I want them to lead."

I nodded, then asked quietly, "And what would that give you?"

The question landed differently. Michael paused. He noticed a tightening in his chest, a flicker of unease. After a long silence, he said, almost reluctantly, "It would make me feel successful—like I'm doing my job as a leader."

I smiled gently. "So, your intention isn't only to empower them. It's also to prove something—perhaps to yourself."

The realization was unmistakable. His initiative, though well-meaning, was still organized around him—around being seen as a good leader, around validating his worth through others' success. Beneath the language of service lived a quieter desire for self-approval.

That evening, Michael sat alone, reflecting. He noticed how much energy he spent managing perception, maintaining control, and trying to get leadership "right." For the first time, he saw that his effort to empower others was still organized around his own need for validation.

The next morning, he made a quiet shift. Instead of trying to empower others, he chose to trust them—and himself—enough to remain present rather than control.

In meetings, he stopped offering premature solutions. He asked open, penetrating questions and allowed silence to do its work. He delegated decisions fully, holding people accountable while resisting the urge to rescue when discomfort arose. It felt unfamiliar, even risky. But slowly, something changed.

Within weeks, the energy in the company shifted. Leaders became more confident and proactive. Conversations grew more candid. Creative ideas resurfaced. As Michael released the need to be the source of success, success began to emerge through the team.

Looking back, he reflected:

"I thought empowerment was about giving others control. But real empowerment began when I stopped trying to prove myself."

Through awareness, Michael's intention shifted. The same actions—meetings, projects, delegation—now carried a different energy. What had once been an effort to *validate himself* shifted to an authentic desire to *see others flourish.*

And that shift—invisible but profound—changed everything. Once intention is clarified, attention becomes the means through which it is expressed.

## The Energy of Attention

If intention is the seed of creation, attention is the sunlight that helps it grow. Without attention, even the purest intention remains dormant, a potential unexpressed.

But when we focus our awareness deliberately, we direct energy. And where energy flows, reality begins to take shape.

Attention is the bridge between the invisible and the visible. It's how intention enters the world.

In every moment, our attention either strengthens alignment with intention—or scatters it.

Most people live with divided attention—thinking about one thing, doing another, emotionally tethered to something else. The result is diluted energy and fragmented impact.

Conscious attention is unified energy, an awareness directed by choice. It's the ability to be fully present with what we are doing, without being pulled by distraction or driven by reactivity.

In this state, our nervous system becomes coherent, our mind clear, and our energy aligned. Modern neuroscience shows that repeated patterns of attention strengthen corresponding neural pathways. This is a phenomenon known as neuroplasticity. What we consistently focus on, we reinforce. Over time, attention sculpts perception, emotion, and behavior.[1]

In leadership, this means that the quality of our attention defines not only our perception but also the culture we create around us.

Research in social neuroscience suggests that emotional states and attentional patterns are socially contagious. Leaders who are scattered tend to amplify fragmentation; leaders who are grounded tend to stabilize the field around them.[2]When our intention is clear, and our attention steady, coherence arises—in the mind, in relationships, and in the systems we lead.

Researchers studying heart rate variability have identified physiological coherence states in which the nervous system becomes more synchronized. In these states, clarity of thinking and emotional regulation improve, and our presence becomes more stable under pressure.[3]

In this state, our presence itself becomes a stabilizing force for others.

Attention and presence are deeply related, yet distinct.

Attention is directional—it focuses awareness like a beam of light.

Presence is dimensional—it is the space within which that light moves.

Attention connects us to the moment; presence connects us to ourselves in the moment.

Or as I often remind leaders, attention anchors us in the moment; presence anchors the moment in us.

When attention arises from presence, it carries a different quality: calm, attuned, and coherent. Presence is what transforms focused attention into a healing force.

In leadership, we often speak about *executive presence,* which is the ability to command a room with calm confidence and authority. Yet true presence has nothing to do with performance or appearance. It is not something we project; it is something we *inhabit.*

When attention is fragmented—divided between what we're saying, how we're being perceived, and what outcome we want—our energy feels scattered. People may hear our words, but they don't feel our essence.

Presence arises when attention returns home, when awareness settles fully into the body, breath, and moment.

In that state, there is no need to perform confidence; it emanates naturally. Others feel it is not because we are controlling the space, but because we are anchored in it.

This is the essence of real executive presence: attention stabilized by presence and awareness rooted in being. Attention is not control; it's connection.

To focus consciously is not to strain or fixate, but to listen deeply to what life is presenting now.

It is to offer our full presence to the moment—to a conversation, a decision, a problem—and to respond from stillness rather than impulse.

This is why conscious leaders pause before they act. They understand that a few seconds of intentional awareness can transform the quality of an entire meeting, negotiation, or strategy session. They know that presence precedes precision, that who they are being shapes what they are doing.

Attention also reveals what is unresolved within us. Whatever we resist internally will keep demanding our attention until it is seen. By meeting that discomfort with awareness instead of avoidance, we free the energy it holds. That released energy then becomes available for creativity and service.

In practice, this means learning to stay with what is—whether that's silence, tension, or uncertainty—long enough to perceive what's really happening beneath the surface.

In that space of patient attention, intuition awakens. We begin to see possibilities that were invisible when we were rushing or reacting.

Attention is the expression of presence, like the way consciousness touches the world. When our presence is steady, our attention becomes clear, and our leadership gains quiet power.

Through the marriage of intention, attention, and presence, we lead not by effort but by energy—not by control, but by alignment.

When attention is aligned with conscious intention, leadership becomes less about managing outcomes and more about generating coherence, both within self, within others, and within the field we all share.

Conscious leaders learn to master this inner technology: They set clear intentions, focus their attention, and allow creation to unfold through aligned action. In that alignment, effort turns to ease, and purpose turns into presence.

## When Intention Meets Impact

Every intention eventually meets the reality of its impact. This meeting is where consciousness matures—where our inner clarity is tested by outer experience. Even the most sincere intentions can cause harm when awareness fades.

We can have the right idea, the right plan, and even the right intention, and still create outcomes that conflict with what we hoped for.

This is the paradox of intention: it may begin pure but become distorted by attachment to goals, pride, or unconscious bias. When that happens, the gap between **intention and impact** widens.

A leader may intend to "push for excellence," yet unknowingly create an environment of fear and burnout. Another may intend to "protect the team," but in doing so, shield them from the growth that comes through challenge. What starts as drive becomes pressure; what begins as care turns into control.

The problem is rarely in the intention itself—it's in the *unexamined energy* behind it.

When we identify with our intention ("I meant well, therefore I am right"), we stop being curious about its impact. We defend instead of listen. We justify instead of learn.

Conscious leaders understand that good intentions are not enough. Awareness must stay alive throughout the entire process of creation—from the spark of intention to the ripple of impact.

They practice humility: the willingness to examine how their actions land, not just how they were meant. This humility turns leadership into a living dialogue rather than a static plan.

It allows intention to evolve through feedback, experience, and reflection.

Awareness keeps intention honest. The moment we realize our impact is misaligned, we have a choice—not to retreat into guilt or justification, but to return to awareness, to reconnect to essence, and to adjust. This is how intention matures: through humility, reflection, and correction.

Good intentions are like seeds: they need constant tending. Without awareness, weeds of ego and fear take root, and even the best soil becomes tangled. But when awareness and humility work together, intention stays clear and alive.

Conscious leadership isn't about getting it right every time. It's about staying awake and being willing to learn, realign, and grow as life reveals more of itself through us.

## Living with Intention

Conscious intention is not something we set once; it is something we live moment by moment.

It is less about making declarations and more about maintaining connection—to essence, to purpose, and to the living intelligence that moves through us. This is not a philosophical ideal. It is a lived discipline that shows up in meetings, decisions, conversations, and moments of pressure.

To live with intention is to bring awareness into the ordinary. It is pausing before speaking, breathing before reacting, and feeling before deciding. It is remembering that every action, no matter how small, carries energy—and that energy leaves a trace in the world.

When we live intentionally, we no longer move out of habit; we move out of choice. We notice the subtle impulses that precede our words and actions, and we align them with what truly matters.

The question shifts from *"What do I need to do?"* to *"Who am I being as I do it?"*

This awareness brings a quiet power. It replaces striving with participation, with a sense that we are collaborating with life rather than controlling it.

Our intentions become living frequencies that shape our relationships, our organizations, and the atmosphere around us.

Living with intention doesn't mean constant perfection; it means continuous return. It is the practice of realignment—of coming home, again and again, to essence. Sometimes that return happens through stillness, sometimes through feedback, sometimes through courage or surrender. Each time we return, we refine the field of energy through which we lead.

In this way, conscious intention becomes a rhythm—an inhale and exhale of awareness. We inhale to connect inwardly; we exhale to express outwardly. We listen, act, adjust, and begin again.

Over time, this rhythm turns into an embodied way of being. Our doing flows naturally from our being. Decisions feel clear, communication feels honest, and results unfold with ease because the energy behind them is coherent.

To live with intention is to make each moment an act of creation. It is to live awake, being aware of the invisible preparation behind every visible outcome. It is to align with essence, breathe with awareness, and act with purpose. It is to live as the artist of our own energy, painting each day with conscious awareness, humility, and love.

And when we live this way, leadership stops being a role and becomes a presence—a quiet, radiant force that elevates everything it touches.

## TAKEAWAYS

- ✦ Intention precedes creation. Every word, action, and outcome carries the energy of its origin.
- ✦ The energy behind the doing shapes the quality of the result. What we create reflects the consciousness we bring to it.
- ✦ Awareness purifies intention. Seeing our hidden motives with compassion dissolves distortion.
- ✦ Ego-driven intention seeks to control; essence-driven intention seeks to express.
- ✦ Desire arises from lack; intention arises from wholeness. One grasps to get, the other allows to express.
- ✦ When intention aligns with essence, effort turns to flow. Life begins to move through us rather than by us.
- ✦ Attention amplifies intention. Where attention goes, energy flows—and presence turns attention into power.
- ✦ True presence is awareness anchored in being. Executive presence is not performance, but calm authority without force.
- ✦ There can be a gap between intention and impact. Good intentions are not enough. Awareness must stay alive from the spark of intention to the ripple of impact.
- ✦ Humility turns leadership into a living dialogue. Feedback refines intention; awareness keeps it honest.
- ✦ Living with intention is a daily return. We realign through breath, awareness, and choice, moment by moment.
- ✦ To lead consciously is to live intentionally. When our being and doing become one, leadership becomes art.

## PRACTICES

The value of intention lies not in understanding it, but in living it. The following practices invite you to bring greater awareness to your intentions throughout the day and align your attention and actions with what matters most.

### 1. The Morning Alignment

Each morning, before checking messages or diving into tasks, take a few quiet minutes to align your energy.

- Sit comfortably and bring attention to your breath.
- Ask: *"What is my true intention for this day?"*

  Notice what arises—perhaps to serve, to create, to learn, or to bring calm.

  Let that intention settle into your body, not as a thought but as a felt presence.

  Throughout the day, return to it before key interactions or decisions.

  This simple practice sets the energetic tone for everything that follows.

### 2. The Pause of Awareness

Before responding to an important email, making a high-stakes decision, or entering a consequential meeting, pause for one conscious breath.

Ask inwardly: *"What energy is moving through me right now?"*

Is it fear, pressure, eagerness, or clarity?

If the energy feels tight or reactive, take another breath and reconnect to essence, to the part of you that acts from love, truth, or service.

Then respond.

This two-second pause can transform unconscious reaction into conscious creation.

**3. The Mirror of Impact**

At the end of each week, reflect on the gap—if any between your intentions and your impact.

- *Where did your actions align with your deeper intention?*
- *Where did they create outcomes or emotional effects that you did not intend?*

  Instead of judging, stay curious.

  Ask gently:

  *"What did I miss along the way—in myself, in others, or in the situation?"*

  *"What energy was shaping my actions in those moments?"*

Let the answers surface without analysis. This is not about blame or perfection, but about expanding awareness.

This practice refines intention through lived experience and strengthens humility, discernment, and energetic coherence over time.

**4. The Attention Reset**

Once or twice a day, notice where your attention is.

*Is it scattered, multitasking, or present?*

Bring your awareness back to your body and breath—even for ten seconds.

Feel your feet, your hands, your heartbeat.

As attention returns to the body, presence returns to you.

From that state, re-engage with whatever you were doing.

This brief reset reconnects intention, attention, and presence; the inner technology of conscious leadership.

**5. The Evening Realignment**

Before sleep, take a few minutes to reflect:

- *What intention guided me today?*
- *Where did I act from alignment, and where did I drift into striving or control?*
- *What lesson or awareness can I carry into tomorrow?*

  End by silently affirming:

  *May my intentions be clear, my awareness steady, and my actions aligned with truth.*

This closes the day with coherence and prepares the inner field for renewal.

## CHAPTER 2

# Conscious Breath

*Feelings come and go like clouds in a windy sky.*
*Conscious breathing is my anchor.*
—Thích Nhất Hạnh

Breath is always present. Before thought, before emotion, before reaction, there is breath. It moves automatically, without instruction or effort. Yet unlike most bodily processes, breath is also consciously accessible—something we can feel, influence, and regulate. This is what makes breath such a powerful lever for leaders: it sits at the intersection of consciousness and physiology, awareness and action.

This is where conscious leadership deepens. Leadership does not begin with words, decisions, or strategies. It begins with state. The inner condition from which a leader speaks, listens, and acts shapes everything that follows: tone, trust, clarity, and impact. Two leaders can say the same words in the same situation and produce entirely different outcomes, depending on the state they are in when they speak them. Breath is the fastest and most direct way to influence that state.

Breathing patterns send powerful signals to the nervous system. When breath is shallow, hurried, or constricted, the body signals urgency, threat, or control. When breath is slow, full, and grounded, the body signals safety, presence, and availability. Long before the mind catches up, the breath has already set the tone. Most leaders attempt to regulate their behavior. Few attend to the state from which that behavior arises.

Conscious breathing brings attention to the source. It allows leaders to notice when they are operating from contraction rather than clarity, from reactivity rather than choice. Through breath, leaders learn to interrupt unconscious patterns—not by suppression or force, but by returning to presence. This is not a wellness practice. It is a leadership discipline.

In moments of pressure, conflict, or uncertainty, the breath becomes an anchor—steadying attention, widening perception, and creating the inner space necessary for wise action. Through conscious breath, leaders learn to regulate themselves first, so they can meet others with steadiness rather than spillover.

Breath does not eliminate emotion. It creates the capacity to be with it. As awareness settles into the body through breath, leaders gain access to clarity, emotional intelligence, and intuition. Decisions become less reactive. Listening deepens. Presence becomes tangible. From this regulated inner state, leadership shifts from management to mastery.

Conscious breath is the foundation of self-regulation. And self-regulation is the foundation of conscious leadership.

## Breath as the Foundation of Self-Mastery

Breath is the most accessible gateway to self-mastery.

While leaders often focus on developing skills—communication, strategy, decision-making—their effectiveness is ultimately constrained by something more fundamental: their capacity to regulate their inner state. No amount of technical competence can compensate for a leader who is overwhelmed, reactive, or unconsciously driven by stress or fear. Breath operates at this foundational level.

Because breathing patterns are directly linked to the nervous system, they influence how safe, alert, or threatened the body feels in any given moment. When the body senses threat, perception narrows, emotions intensify, and behavior becomes reactive. When the body senses safety, perception widens, attention stabilizes, and choice becomes possible. Long before a leader speaks or acts, this physiological reality has already shaped the field. This is why breath matters in leadership.

Self-mastery is not about controlling emotion or suppressing reaction. It is about developing the capacity to remain present and responsive under pressure. Conscious breath trains this capacity by bringing awareness to the moment when an automatic reaction begins—and offering a way to interrupt it before it becomes behavior.

For leaders, this has immediate implications. Meetings, negotiations, and difficult conversations are rarely derailed by a lack of intelligence or preparation. They are derailed when internal state overwhelms awareness. A constricted breath often precedes a sharp tone. A rushed breath precedes a premature decision. An absent breath precedes disconnection. Conscious breathing restores choice at precisely these moments.

By learning to notice and regulate the breath, leaders gain access to a stabilizing inner reference point—one that is available regardless of circumstance. This inner stability does not slow leadership down; it sharpens it. From a regulated state, leaders can respond with clarity rather than reflex, and with presence rather than performance.

Over time, the way leaders operate under pressure reshapes the body itself. Under sustained pressure, many leaders unknowingly adopt shallow, constrained breathing patterns that become normalized as "just how things are." This chronic narrowing of breath subtly reinforces vigilance, urgency, and tension, even in moments that do not require it. Conscious breath restores access to a fuller baseline, not by fixing stress in the moment, but by retraining the body to recognize safety again. In this way, breath becomes a practice of long-term self-mastery, not merely short-term regulation.

Self-mastery begins not with effort, but with awareness. Breath is where that awareness becomes embodied.

## Breath, the Nervous System, and State

Breath is the most direct interface between consciousness and the nervous system.

Much of human behavior is shaped not by deliberate choice, but by the body's automatic assessment of safety and threat. This assessment happens continuously, below conscious awareness, through the autonomic nervous system.[5]

When the nervous system perceives danger—whether physical, emotional, or social—it shifts the body into a state of protection. Heart rate increases, muscles tense, attention narrows, and behavior becomes oriented toward defense or control. Leaders operate inside this physiological reality at all times.

Under pressure, the nervous system does not distinguish between a physical threat and a psychological one. A tense meeting, an unexpected challenge, or perceived loss of control can trigger the same survival responses as a more obvious danger. When this happens, even experienced leaders may find themselves reacting in ways that feel misaligned with their values or intentions.

Breath plays a central role in this process. Breathing patterns send powerful signals to the nervous system. Shallow, rapid breathing reinforces a state of urgency or threat. Slow, steady breathing activates the parasympathetic response, signaling safety and stability.[4]

This shift does not eliminate challenges, but it changes how they are met—opening access to clarity, empathy, and perspective. This is why breath is such a powerful regulatory tool.

Because breathing can be consciously influenced, it becomes one of the fastest ways leaders can shift their internal state. By slowing the breath, lengthening the exhale, or bringing attention to its rhythm, leaders can directly influence their internal state. This intervention occurs faster than cognitive reframing and is more reliable than willpower. It works not by suppressing emotion, but by stabilizing the physiological ground from which emotion arises.

From this regulated state, perception widens. The mind becomes less reactive and more discerning. Leaders are better able to listen, to sense what is happening beneath the surface, and to respond rather than react. The same situation can feel entirely different depending on whether it is experienced through a constricted or a regulated nervous system.

Breath does not solve problems. It creates the conditions for wise problem-solving to become possible.

For conscious leaders, understanding this relationship is essential. The quality of leadership presence—calm or anxious, open or defensive, grounded or scattered—is shaped long before words are spoken. Breath is one of the few levers leaders can use, in real time, to influence that presence from the inside out.

## Emotional Regulation and Presence

Emotional regulation is not the absence of emotion. It is the capacity to remain present with it.

Leadership regularly places people in situations that activate strong emotions: frustration, anxiety, urgency, fear, and disappointment. These emotional responses are not signs of weakness; they are natural signals arising from the nervous system. The challenge is not that emotions arise, but that when they are unregulated, they unconsciously drive behavior.

This is where breath becomes decisive. When emotional intensity increases, the breath often becomes shallow, rapid, or held. This physiological shift amplifies emotional charge and narrows perception, making it difficult to listen, reflect, or choose wisely. Leaders may speak too quickly, react defensively, or push for resolution prematurely—not because they intend to, but because their internal state has overtaken awareness.

Conscious breathing interrupts this pattern at its source. By directing attention to the breath during emotionally charged moments, leaders create a pause—not of action, but of reactivity. This pause restores presence. It allows emotion to be felt without being enacted, acknowledged without being projected. From this place, leaders are far more likely to respond in ways that align with their values and intentions.

## Why Breath Works Before Thought

Leaders often believe they can think their way back into clarity. Neuroscience suggests otherwise. Under pressure, the nervous system shifts into protective modes that narrow perception, accelerate judgment, and prioritize speed over discernment. In these states, access to higher-order reasoning, empathy, and ethical restraint is reduced—not because leaders lack capability, but because the body is signaling threat.

Breath offers a direct pathway back to regulation because it is one of the few voluntary actions that immediately influences involuntary systems. Subtle changes in breathing rhythm affect heart rate variability, emotional reactivity, and the balance between activation and recovery in the nervous system.[6] When breath slows and deepens, the system receives a signal of safety; when breath becomes rhythmic and intentional, energy can mobilize without tipping into aggression.

This is why breath precedes insight. It restores access to discernment before decisions are made, words are spoken, or power is exercised. Conscious breathing does not eliminate intensity or urgency—it refines them, allowing leaders to act from presence rather than impulse.

## Two Ways Leaders Work with Breath

Conscious breathing is about learning how to meet different leadership moments with the appropriate internal state. At a fundamental level, leaders work with breath in two ways: to stabilize presence and to mobilize clean energy.

Effective leadership requires knowing when to settle the system and when to mobilize it. Conscious breath allows leaders to do both—intentionally.

## 1. Breath for Stabilizing Presence (Grounding Under Pressure)

### Leadership function

To prevent reactive spillover before speaking, deciding, correcting, or entering high-stakes interactions.

When to use

- Before difficult conversations
- When irritation, urgency, or judgment is present
- Before exercising authority or giving feedback

### Practice

- Place one hand on the lower belly.
- Inhale slowly through the nose for approximately 4 seconds, allowing the belly to expand.
- Exhale gently through the nose or mouth for approximately 6 to 8 seconds, allowing the body to soften.
- Repeat for three to five cycles, maintaining ease rather than effort.

### What this trains over time

- Nervous system stability under pressure
- Reduced impulsivity
- The ability to pause without losing momentum

As leaders practice this form of breathing, they often notice subtle but meaningful shifts. The voice slows. The body softens. The urge to force or rush loosens. Clarity returns without effort. This is not about calming down. It is about becoming available to act without distortion.

## 2. Breath for Mobilizing Energy (Meeting Challenge Without Force)

### Leadership function

To access vitality, alertness, and forward movement without tipping into aggression or urgency.

When to use

- Before demanding meetings or presentations
- When energy is low, but clarity is needed
- When leadership requires visibility, decisiveness, or courage

### Practice

- Sit or stand upright, spine long, chest open without strain.

- Inhale and exhale deeply through the nose for approximately two–three seconds each, maintaining an even, rhythmic pace.
- Continue for thirty to sixty seconds, keeping the breath smooth and connected.
- Stop immediately if lightheadedness or tension arises.

### What this trains over time

- Clean activation without anxiety
- Presence with power
- Energy that is focused rather than frantic

With practice, leaders notice a different quality of energy emerging. Alertness increases. Posture aligns. Confidence arises without tension. This is not a calming breath. It is a centering breath that supports action without force or aggression.

At first glance, these practices may appear deceptively simple. Yet their effectiveness lies precisely in their simplicity. Research in neuroscience and physiology shows that breathing patterns directly influence emotional regulation, attention, and impulse control. Small changes in how we breathe can produce immediate changes in how we perceive, decide, and relate.

Jack, a CEO I worked with, offers a clear illustration of how this shift plays out in practice.

Jack was intelligent, driven, and deeply committed to results. He held high standards and moved fast. Yet in moments of pressure—especially when timelines slipped, or expectations were not met—his frustration surfaced quickly. His tone sharpened. His body tightened. Meetings grew tense.

Over time, this had a cost.

Team members began to filter what they brought to him. Difficult conversations were delayed or avoided. Problems were softened before they reached his desk—or escalated too late. In meetings, people spoke carefully, watching his reactions rather than contributing fully. Execution slowed, not because the team lacked capability, but because energy was spent managing the emotional field rather than the work itself.

To Jack, his reactions felt justified. He cared deeply. He wanted excellence. What he hadn't seen was how his internal state—unexpressed irritation, unprocessed urgency, underlying impatience—was shaping the environment around him. Without intending to, he was creating pressure that narrowed thinking and reduced trust.

As we worked together, Jack began practicing a simple discipline: noticing his breath at the first sign of irritation. He didn't try to calm himself down or change the situation. He simply slowed his breathing and stayed present with the sensation in his body before speaking.

The shift was subtle—but powerful.

By regulating his breath, Jack regulated his state. His words softened without losing clarity. His presence became steadier. He still addressed issues directly—but without the edge that triggered defensiveness. Over time, his team began to respond differently. Conversations opened. Risks were surfaced earlier. Trust increased. Accountability improved—not because Jack pushed harder, but because the environment felt safer and more coherent.

Nothing about Jack's role or expectations changed. What changed was the state from which he led.

This is the quiet power of conscious breath. Emotional regulation through breath does not make leaders passive or detached.

On the contrary, it enables firmness without aggression, clarity without force, and decisiveness without domination. Presence becomes something others can feel—an unspoken signal of stability that allows teams to think, speak, and act more freely.

Breath does not remove emotion. It allows leaders to stay with it—without being ruled by it.

## The Leader as Regulator of State

Whether consciously or not, leaders influence the emotional and energetic state of the environments they engage with.

This is not a matter of personality or intention; it is a function of presence. A leader's inner state—calm or agitated, open or defensive, grounded or scattered—inevitably influences the people around them. Teams attune to this state quickly, often before any words are spoken. Over time, it becomes part of the culture.

Conscious leaders understand this responsibility. Regulating state does not mean controlling others' emotions, suppressing one's own feelings, or maintaining artificial calm. It means taking responsibility for the internal conditions from which leadership is exercised. Breath is central to this responsibility because it is the primary means by which leaders regulate themselves in real time.

When leaders arrive dysregulated—rushed, tense, reactive—the field tightens. Conversations narrow. Creativity contracts. People protect themselves rather than contribute fully. When leaders arrive regulated—present, grounded, and available—the field opens. Trust increases. Listening deepens. The system becomes more intelligent.

Breath anchors leadership in the body. It allows leaders to maintain urgency without losing presence, sensing when pressure begins to trigger control or unconscious patterns, and recalibrating before that drift shapes behavior. Over time, this capacity becomes embodied. Regulation is no longer something leaders do; it is something they are known for.

This is especially important in moments of uncertainty or stress. When external conditions are volatile, the leader's inner stability becomes a reference point for others. Teams look to the leader not for certainty of outcome, but for steadiness of presence. Breath supports this steadiness quietly, without drawing attention to itself. Over time, a leader's regulated—or dysregulated—state becomes the emotional baseline of the team.

To lead consciously is to recognize that leadership is always transmitted, not just expressed. By tending to their own state through conscious breath, leaders influence the system without force. They create environments where people feel safe enough to think clearly, speak honestly, and act responsibly. In this way, breath becomes an ethical practice because it prevents unconscious spillover.

## Breath, Clarity, and Creative Intelligence

Much of what leaders experience as mental overload or lack of focus is not a failure of thinking, but a consequence of internal noise. When the body is tense or agitated, attention fragments. Thoughts race. Perception narrows. In this state, even highly capable leaders struggle to see situations clearly or sense what truly matters. Conscious breath quiets this noise at its source.

By stabilizing the nervous system, breath creates the conditions for mental clarity—not by forcing concentration, but by reducing internal interference. As the breath slows and deepens, attention becomes steadier. The mind settles. Leaders regain access to a wider field of perception, where nuance, context, and possibility become visible again.

Clarity, in this sense, is not effortful. It is revealed when distraction falls away.

Much of what limits creativity is not a lack of intelligence, but the persistence of habitual thought. Over time, leaders accumulate assumptions, self-referential narratives, and conditioned ways of interpreting reality. These patterns are efficient, but they are also constraining. When left unquestioned, they narrow perception and make genuinely new possibilities difficult to see.

Neuroscience offers a useful lens here. Research on the brain's default mode network suggests that much of our mental activity is devoted to maintaining familiar narratives about who we are, what is possible, and how the world works.[7] While this function is valuable, it can also confine leaders within repetitive loops of thought, especially under pressure. Conscious breath helps loosen this grip.

As the nervous system settles and attention returns to the body, breath creates distance from automatic narratives without suppressing them. Identification softens. Mental chatter quiets. In this space, perception widens. Leaders become more capable of noticing what they had previously overlooked and sensing possibilities that do not fit established patterns.

This is where creative intelligence emerges. Insight often arises not as a product of effort, but as a recognition—something that was present but obscured by noise. Many leaders discover that when they stop pushing for answers and instead stabilize their state through breath, clarity surfaces naturally. What becomes clear is not only *what* to do, but *when* and *how* to do it.

More intensive breath practices have long been used in contemplative and therapeutic settings to access non-ordinary states of awareness, where deeply ingrained patterns can temporarily loosen or dissolve. While such practices are neither necessary nor appropriate for everyone, they point to an important truth: breath has the capacity to shift perception by interrupting habitual modes of consciousness.

For conscious leaders, the invitation is not to seek extraordinary states, but to cultivate steady access to clarity in ordinary moments. Through simple, consistent attention to breath, leaders learn to step out of conditioned thinking and meet complexity with fresh eyes.

Breath does not generate intelligence. It clears the channel through which intelligence flows.

In this way, conscious breathing supports leadership that is not only calm and regulated, but perceptive and responsive. From clarity arises wise choice. From a wise choice, coherent action becomes possible. From this regulated inner state, leaders are prepared to listen more deeply and choose more wisely.

## TAKEAWAYS

- Breath is the foundation of self-regulation. Conscious breath is the most direct and reliable way leaders can influence their inner state in real time, restoring presence before thought or action.
- State precedes behavior. Leadership effectiveness is shaped less by skill or intention than by the internal condition from which decisions, communication, and actions arise.
- Breath regulates the nervous system, not emotions directly. By stabilizing physiology, breath creates the conditions in which emotions can be felt without unconsciously driving behavior.
- Leaders transmit state, whether consciously or not. Through breath, leaders learn to take responsibility for the emotional and relational field they shape—by regulating themselves rather than controlling others.
- Clarity emerges when internal noise quiets. Conscious breathing loosens habitual thought patterns and clears the channel through which discernment becomes possible.
- Breath supports creative intelligence and insight. By softening identification with habitual narratives and expanding perception, conscious breath allows leaders to access intuition, fresh perspectives, and wiser timing in complex situations.
- Breath supports presence, not avoidance. It does not eliminate emotion or uncertainty but enables leaders to remain grounded and responsive within them.
- Conscious breath is a core discipline of self-mastery. By cultivating awareness of breath, leaders develop the capacity to meet pressure with steadiness, choice, and coherence, supporting every other dimension of conscious leadership.

## PRACTICES

The following practices are designed to help you integrate the principles of conscious breathing into daily life. Experiment with them regularly and notice how greater awareness of the breath influences your state, presence, and responses.

### Regulating State Before Action

Before entering a meeting, conversation, or decision that matters, pause for one minute. Bring attention to your breath without changing it at first. Then gently slow the exhale, allowing it to become slightly longer and more complete than the inhale. Feel the body settle before you speak or act.

*What state am I bringing into this moment—and is it the state I want to transmit?*

### Interrupting Reactivity in Real Time

When irritation, urgency, defensiveness, or emotional charge begins to arise, shift attention from the narrative in your mind to the physical sensation of breathing in the body. Stay with the sensation of the breath for two or three full cycles before responding.

*Can I remain present with this feeling without letting it drive my next move?*

### The Physiological Sigh (Rapid State Reset)[8]

When stress or pressure spikes and a quick reset is needed, take a slow inhale through the nose. Before exhaling, take a second, shorter sip of air to fully expand the lungs. Then exhale slowly and completely through the mouth. Repeat once or twice to allow the body to settle.

*What becomes available when my body settles before my mind reacts?*

### Breath as an Anchor for Presence

During conversations where listening, trust, or emotional safety matter, periodically return attention to the breath in your body—especially the belly or chest—while remaining open and engaged with the other person.

*Am I truly here, or am I preparing my response?*

### Clearing the Channel for Insight

When facing complexity or uncertainty, step away from the problem temporarily. Take five to ten slow, steady breaths, allowing attention to settle into the body. Do not seek an answer. Let clarity arise on its own timing.

*What becomes visible when I stop forcing resolution?*

## Closing the Day with Awareness

At the end of the day, take two minutes to notice how you are breathing. Without judgment, observe whether the breath is shallow, held, or relaxed. Allow it to deepen naturally as you release the day.

*What state am I carrying forward—and what am I ready to let go of?*

## CHAPTER 3

# Conscious Stance

*Be still like a grounded mountain, and flow like a living river.*

—Adapted from Lao Tzu

Before we take our first step, we must know how to stand.

Our stance—physically, mentally, emotionally, and spiritually—shapes how we meet the world. It is the invisible foundation of leadership, the ground from which all action arises. Every leader has a stance, whether they are aware of it or not.

Some stand firm but rigid. Others are light but unstable. Some collapse under pressure; others push harder to maintain control. Conscious stance is neither stiffness nor passivity. It is the embodiment of stability, openness, and flow—the alignment of body, mind, and essence in the present moment.

To stand consciously is to be fully present in one's space—grounded, open, and ready. It is to meet life as it is: steady yet responsive, rooted yet adaptable. When we are centered in this way, our energy communicates before our words do. People feel our presence, not just our position.

Conscious stance begins in the body. The way we hold ourselves reflects how we hold our lives. If the breath anchors awareness, the stance anchors being. In moments of uncertainty or pressure, returning to the body—feeling the ground beneath the feet, sensing the spine's alignment, softening unnecessary tension—can instantly reconnect us to stability and presence.

But stance is more than posture. It is also the orientation of the mind and heart. Do we meet challenges with openness or resistance? Do we listen to understand, or to defend? Our stance reveals where we are leading from—fear or trust, control or flow, ego or essence.

When we are misaligned within, our actions carry strain and fragmentation. When we are aligned—grounded in awareness and integrity—our presence steadies, our words become coherent, and our decisions grow clearer.

Conscious leadership begins with this simple truth: before we can lead others, we must learn to stand well within ourselves. To stand consciously is to stand in contact with something deeper than circumstance, a ground of being that does not waver with external conditions. From this ground, leadership becomes less about forcing outcomes and more about shaping coherence, less about control and more about clarity. It is from this inner posture that true power, compassion, and discernment emerge.

Stance is revealed most clearly under pressure. When circumstances tighten, deadlines compress, or authority is challenged, stance determines whether a leader responds with grounded clarity or unconscious force. In these moments, true power is not expressed through pressure or control, but through alignment. Force may compel compliance, but it erodes trust. A conscious stance generates authority without aggression—because it is rooted in presence rather than fear.

## The Body as the Anchor of Consciousness

Leadership begins in the body.

Before vision, before strategy, before speech, there is stance. The body is the first place where consciousness takes form. It reflects our inner state more honestly than words ever can. When the body is tense, the mind narrows; when the body softens, awareness widens.[11] To change how we stand is to change how we think, perceive, and lead.

The body anchors presence. When we feel the ground beneath our feet, the weight of the body balanced and the breath flowing freely, we send a signal to the nervous system: *I am safe*. Safety is the foundation of awareness.[9] Only from a grounded state can clarity, empathy, and discernment fully engage. This is why a centered leader can shift the tone of a room without saying a word—their body becomes a stabilizing reference point that others unconsciously attune to.

Modern research in embodiment and somatic psychology echoes what ancient wisdom has long known: leadership is embodied before it is articulated.[10] Our nervous system does not live only in the brain; it expresses itself through posture, breath, and muscle tone.

When leaders are disconnected from their bodies—living primarily from the neck up—they lose access to this intelligence. They may speak eloquently, yet communicate tension, reactive urgency, or anxiety through subtle contraction. Teams feel this dissonance immediately.

Conscious stance begins when we return home to the body—when we allow the body to orient the mind back to the present moment. From this grounded place, leadership shifts from reaction to response, from control to coherence.

Stance is the bridge between inner state and outer impact. Long before people hear what we say, they feel how we are. Presence is transmitted faster than language. A misaligned stance creates misaligned outcomes; an integrated stance creates integrated impact. How we stand reveals how we will lead.

Integrity becomes visible through stance. Integrity is not only a moral principle; it is an embodied condition in which inner experience, outer expression, and deeper values are aligned. When a leader stands in integrity, there is a felt coherence—words, tone, and presence match. Trust arises naturally, without effort.

When words and inner experience are misaligned, stance carries the truth. People may not consciously name the discrepancy, but they feel it. Trust erodes not because of what the leader says, but because their presence reveals what remains unspoken. In this way, conscious stance becomes an ethical posture—an embodied commitment to stand in truth.

This is where authentic authority arises. A leader grounded in their body does not need to assert power to be felt as powerful. Their stability creates gravity. Their presence sets the tone. Decisions carry weight not because they are imposed, but because they emerge from coherence. This form of authority does not demand attention; it commands respect quietly, through alignment rather than force.

From this foundation emerges the distinction between force and personal power.

## Force vs Personal Power

In leadership, force and personal power are often mistaken for one another. Both can produce results, especially under pressure, but they arise from very different inner stances and leave very different traces in the people and systems they touch.

Force arises from contraction. It is driven by reactive urgency, fear, or the need to control outcomes. It tightens the body, narrows perception, and pushes against resistance. Force may compel compliance, but it also generates tension, defensiveness, and quiet withdrawal. Results may be achieved, but at a cost to trust, creativity, and long-term coherence.

Personal power arises from alignment. It is grounded, spacious, and internally stable. Rather than pushing against others, it holds its center and allows clarity to emerge. A leader connected to personal power does not need to dominate or convince. Their presence itself carries weight.

Strength, in this sense, is not aggression. It is stability. Not defiance, but the capacity to remain open and uncollapsed under pressure. This kind of strength creates safety rather than tension. It anchors the room without effort.

Force is brittle. It depends on circumstances, positional authority, or external pressure. When conditions change, it fractures. Personal power is resilient. It comes from coherence—between body, values, intention, and action—and remains available even in uncertainty or conflict.

When a leader embodies personal power as a conscious stance, their presence steadies others naturally. Conversations deepen. Reactivity softens. Decisions land with clarity rather than pressure. Personal power is not something a leader projects outward; it is something they stand within.

From this stance, leadership no longer relies on control to create movement. Direction emerges. Authority is felt without being imposed. And influence flows not from force, but from inner alignment made visible.

The difference between force and personal power is not abstract. It reveals itself most clearly under pressure—when authority is challenged, outcomes matter, and the impulse to push is strong. Daniel learned this distinction the hard way.

Daniel was a capable and respected leader—intelligent, driven, and deeply committed to his work. He carried a clear internal vision of how things should unfold, and most of the time, this served him well. But under pressure, something subtle—and consequential—would shift.

When things went wrong—or simply did not match his internal picture—his body reacted instantly. His jaw tightened. His shoulders rose. His breath shortened. His voice sharpened—punchier, faster, edged with impatience. And then the room would feel it: the force.

Daniel wasn't abusive. He wasn't a bully. He wasn't even intentionally unkind. But when reality deviated from his expectations—when timelines slipped, imperfections surfaced, or people failed to anticipate what he assumed was obvious—his stance hardened. His posture locked. His gaze narrowed with intensity. The space around him grew tense.

In meetings, this shift often happened quickly. A concern would be raised, a disagreement voiced, or a perspective offered that felt unnecessary or ill-timed. Daniel's voice would rise, edged with frustration and impatience, and the room would freeze. Listening collapsed. New information could no longer land. His attention narrowed to defending what should be happening.

From the outside, these meetings often appeared productive. Decisions were made. Direction was set. But beneath the surface, something else was occurring. People spoke less. Creativity diminished. Energy drained. What remained was compliance, not commitment.

Daniel felt the cost afterward. The outcome might have been achieved, but the room felt thinner. Conversations grew strained. Trust eroded quietly—not through overt conflict, but through repeated moments of contraction.

What Daniel eventually saw was that the issue was not his intent or his authority. It was his stance.

Under pressure, he was standing in force rather than personal power. His body was leading from tension, not presence. His nervous system was driving the interaction before awareness could intervene. And the room was responding—not to his words, but to his state.

With practice, Daniel learned to notice the early signals: the tightening jaw, the rising shoulders, the shortened breath. These sensations became cues—to pause. To ground. To stand.

In later conversations, when resistance arose, he chose differently. He felt his feet on the ground. He softened his breath. He allowed tension to be present without acting it out. He listened longer. He spoke less. And when he did speak, his voice carried clarity and calm authority.

The decisions were still made. The authority remained intact. But the room stayed alive.

People remained engaged even in disagreement. Conversations retained their vitality. Outcomes landed with far less resistance—not because everyone agreed, but because they felt included, seen, and respected.

Daniel had not become passive. He had not relinquished leadership. He had shifted his stance.

Force arises when pressure pulls us out of ourselves. Personal power emerges when we remain grounded, present, and aligned, especially under strain. Both can produce results. Only one sustains trust.

This is the quiet strength of conscious stance: authority without force, decisiveness without contraction, leadership that steadies rather than dominates.

## Standing in the Middle Way

When force stops working, the question becomes practical:

*How do we stand differently under pressure?*

The answer is not withdrawal, passivity, or compromise. It is centeredness.

Centeredness is the capacity to remain grounded and open at the same time—to hold tension without collapsing or hardening. It is the stance of the Middle Way: neither forceful nor avoidant, neither rigid nor diffuse. From this place, leaders stay present with complexity without being pulled to extremes.

When we lose center, we tend to polarize. We either push to regain control or retreat to avoid discomfort. Both reactions are understandable. Both are costly. Centeredness offers a third option: staying rooted while allowing movement.

Centeredness is not something we think our way into. It is something we inhabit. It is felt as weight settles through the feet, breath slows freely, and the spine stands upright without rigidity. From this embodied center, attention widens. The nervous system stabilizes. Choice becomes available again.

In leadership moments that matter—conflict, uncertainty, resistance—the center becomes the reference point. Instead of reacting to what is happening, the leader stands in relationship to it. This subtle shift changes everything. Authority no longer needs to assert itself. Presence does the work.

The Middle Way does not dilute conviction; it clarifies and strengthens it. A centered leader can hold a clear position without defending it, listen without conceding, and decide without force. This is not neutrality. It is grounded engagement.

Over time, centeredness becomes recognizable. People sense it immediately. Conversations become clearer. Reactivity decreases. Trust increases because the leader remains steady regardless of outcome.

This is the stance that allows leadership to be firm without being brittle, compassionate without losing boundaries, and decisive without being driven by fear.

Centeredness is not a permanent achievement. It is a living practice, especially under pressure, when we are most tempted to leave it.

## Ego-Driven vs. Essence-Driven Stance

At the heart of a conscious stance lies a simple but consequential question:

*Where are we standing from?*

An ego-driven stance arises from identification with role, image, control, or outcome. It is fueled by the need to protect, prove, or preserve a particular version of ourselves or the situation. When ego leads, stance becomes reactive. The body tightens. Attention narrows. The leader feels compelled to manage perception, defend position, or force resolution.

This stance is not malicious. It is human. Ego steps in when we feel threatened—by uncertainty, resistance, or the possibility of failure. But while ego promises control and protection, it delivers contraction. Listening collapses. Creativity diminishes. Relationships become transactional rather than relational.

An essence-driven stance is fundamentally different. It does not originate from fear or self-protection, but from alignment with something deeper and more stable than circumstance. Essence is not personality, role, or achievement. It is the grounded presence beneath them—the part of us that remains intact regardless of outcome.

Essence carries real power. It brings firmness without hardening, connection without merging, and leadership without domination. It is the stance of a leader who is inwardly free and able to act without being driven by fear or attachment.

This distinction is felt moment by moment in the body and in attention. Ego-driven stance often reveals itself through shallow breath, excessive tension, narrowed focus, and an underlying impulse to control or protect. Essence-driven stance, by contrast, is marked by fuller breath, grounded ease, wider awareness, and an orientation toward truth, connection, and creation.

Learning to notice these signals does not require analysis or self-correction. Awareness alone begins to shift stance. Over time, these cues become doorways—ways of recognizing when ego has taken the lead and when it is time to return to a deeper, steadier ground.

One quiet marker of an essence-driven stance is gratitude, not as a sentiment but as an orientation. Gratitude allows a leader to meet reality without resistance. It replaces entitlement with appreciation, impatience with respect, and force with grounded authority. From this stance, challenges are no longer experienced as personal attacks, but as conditions to be engaged with curiosity and intelligence.

This distinction becomes most visible under pressure. When timelines slip, expectations are challenged, or authority is questioned, ego tightens its grip. Essence holds steady, present long enough for a wiser response to emerge.

Standing in essence does not mean abandoning standards, vision, or accountability. It means holding them without attachment to how they must unfold. From this stance, leaders can set boundaries without aggression, make decisions without force, and remain open without losing direction.

Over time, people feel the difference. Ego-driven leadership produces compliance. Essence-driven leadership invites commitment. One relies on pressure; the other on alignment.

Conscious stance is the ongoing practice of noticing when ego has taken the lead and choosing, again and again, to stand somewhere deeper, not by suppressing the ego, but by returning to the essence.

Conscious stance is forged under pressure. Each moment of force offers a choice: tighten and control or return to center. Over time, this choice shapes not only how we lead, but who we become.

## TAKEAWAYS

- ✦ Leadership begins before action. How we stand determines how we lead.
- ✦ Stance is not mindset or posture alone; it is an embodied orientation that shapes perception, choice, and impact.
- ✦ Under pressure, unconscious stance often defaults to force—tightening the body, narrowing attention, and collapsing listening.
- ✦ Personal power does not come from force, but from alignment. It steadies rather than dominates and invites coherence rather than compliance.
- ✦ The body provides early signals. Jaw, breath, shoulders, and attention reveal stance before words do.
- ✦ Centeredness allows leaders to hold tension without hardening or withdrawing. It is the stance of the Middle Way: grounded, open, and responsive.
- ✦ Ego-driven stance seeks control and certainty; essence-driven stance holds clarity without attachment to outcome.
- ✦ Essence is not passive. It sets boundaries without rigidity, connects without merging, and leads without dominating.
- ✦ Teams respond less to what leaders say and more to the stance they embody. Presence shapes trust faster than explanation.
- ✦ Conscious stance is not a destination. It is a practice of returning, especially when pressure invites us to abandon it.

## PRACTICES

Conscious stance is not established through willpower. It is cultivated through repeated returns, especially when pressure pulls us away from ourselves. These practices are invitations to notice, ground, and re-orient how you stand in moments that matter.

### 1. The Return to Ground

Several times a day, particularly before meetings or difficult conversations, pause briefly and feel your feet on the ground. Let your weight settle. Sense gravity supporting you rather than resisting it.

Notice your breath without changing it. Allow it to deepen naturally. This simple return reminds the nervous system that you are here, now, and supported.

Stance begins where contact with the ground is restored.

### 2. The Body Scan Under Pressure

When tension arises, scan the body quickly: jaw, shoulders, belly, feet, breath.

Ask yourself quietly: *Where am I tightening?*

Do not correct or judge—just notice.

Often, awareness alone softens contraction. This practice trains sensitivity to the early signals of force before it takes over.

### 3. Standing Without Pushing

In moments where you feel the urge to assert, convince, or press forward, pause and check your stance.

*Ask: Am I standing, or am I pushing?*

Let your posture realign—upright without rigidity, relaxed without collapse. Speak only after you feel steadiness return. This practice cultivates authority without force.

### 4. Ego-to-Essence Check-In

During challenging interactions, gently inquire inwardly:

- *What am I protecting right now?*
- *What outcome am I attached to?*
- *Can I stand here without needing to control the moment?*

Let the inquiry create space, not analysis. If ego is present, simply notice and return to the body. Essence follows attention.

### 5. Holding the Middle Way

When faced with tension or opposition, resist the pull toward extremes, whether it's domination or withdrawal.

Practice staying in the middle: grounded, open, and engaged. Notice how this stance allows clarity to emerge without urgency.

The Middle Way is not compromise; it is centered presence under pressure.

### 6. After-Action Reflection

At the end of the day, reflect briefly on one moment where your stance mattered.

Ask:

- *Where did I stand from force?*
- *Where did I stand from personal power?*
- *What did my body teach me?*

This reflection builds awareness without self-judgment and deepens learning over time.

## CHAPTER 4

# Conscious Cultivation

*Individuation is the process by which a person becomes a psychological 'in-dividual,' that is, a separate, indivisible unity or "whole."*

—Carl Jung

Conscious leadership is not a moment of inspiration. It is a lifelong practice of becoming.

It is the ongoing cultivation of the inner qualities, patterns, and energies that allow us to lead from essence rather than ego. Cultivation is the quiet architecture behind character—the daily tending of our inner landscape: the soil we stand on, the intentions we plant, the habits we reinforce, and even the patterns that reveal where growth is still needed.

Insight opens the door, but cultivation is what allows us to walk the path.

Every breath we choose, every pause before reacting, every return to center shapes who we are becoming. Leadership is grown through practice, not performance. What we repeatedly reinforce—through attention, habit, and response—gradually forms our nervous system, emotional patterns, intuition, and presence. Over time, these small, often invisible acts accumulate into the leader we embody.

We are entering a world in which artificial intelligence will surpass human beings in memory, speed, and analysis. This shift does not diminish leadership; it clarifies it. As cognition becomes increasingly automated, the inner capacities that cannot be replicated—presence, discernment, integrity, and coherence—move to the center. Cultivation is no longer optional; it is foundational.

Throughout history, mystics, sages, and visionary innovators have pointed to capacities that extend far beyond ordinary cognition; capacities that include profound intuitive knowing, refined perception, extraordinary creative insight, and, in some cases, remarkable physiological and energetic mastery. From qigong masters capable of consciously cultivating and directing life energy, to yogis who can regulate heart rate, metabolism, and bodily states once thought involuntary, to visionaries such as Leonardo da Vinci and Nikola Tesla whose insights arrived ahead of established knowledge, these accounts point to a shared truth: human potential is far more expansive than conventional models suggest.

Cultivation is how that potential is realized—not through force, but through sustained attention, devotion, and the willingness to meet reality without distortion. It is not self-improvement. It is the unfolding of what we are capable of becoming.

This chapter explores cultivation in this deeper sense: how habits shape destiny, how ego patterns are reinforced or softened, and why long-term inner development may be one of the most consequential leadership practices of our time.

## The Long Arc of Becoming

Leadership is not an identity we claim; it is a presence we cultivate.

It emerges slowly, through countless choices and reinforcements. It is shaped less by titles or achievements than by the inner habits that take root within us. Ego seeks transformation through intensity. Essence grows through consistency. Ego longs for the breakthrough—the dramatic shift that changes everything. But conscious leadership is not a moment. It is a path. It is the long arc of becoming someone whose presence, clarity, and integrity can be trusted.

Everything we practice, we become. Everything we repeat, we reinforce. Every day, we are cultivating something, whether it's awareness or distraction, presence or reactivity, openness or defensiveness, essence or ego. Neuroscience and contemplative traditions converge on this truth: the brain and nervous system reorganize themselves through repetition.[12] What is practiced becomes familiar. What is familiar becomes habitual.

If we practice grounding, we become grounded.
If we practice reactivity, we become reactive.
If we practice compassion, we become compassionate.

Cultivation is the bridge between who we are and who we are becoming. It is how intention matures into character and how leadership grows from the inside out.

Still, cultivation is not glamorous. It is quiet. Steady. Repetitive. It lives in invisible moments—in the breath we choose, the stance we return to, the pause we honor instead of reacting. Leadership matures the way a tree grows: not by force, but by nourishment, season after season, until its presence becomes unmistakable.

Cultivation is how leadership becomes not something we do, but something we are.

## The Garden Within

Cultivation begins with recognizing that every leader carries an inner garden, a living ecosystem of thoughts, emotions, energies, habits, patterns, and potentials. This inner landscape is not fixed. It is shaped continuously by what we tend and what we neglect. Like any garden, it grows what is planted and consistently nourished.

We do not cultivate ourselves through force or control; we cultivate by creating conditions in which growth happens naturally.

### Seeds

The seeds of the inner garden are our intentions, values, and commitments. Every sincere intention is a seed of possibility. We plant seeds each time we choose presence over distraction, truth over convenience, compassion over fear, and essence over ego. Seeds do not guarantee growth, but without them, nothing new can emerge.

### Soil

The soil is our stance, the embodied foundation of the nervous system. Grounded soil allows intentions to take root. A reactive, tense, or depleted system cannot nourish growth. When we cultivate grounding, breath, centeredness, and embodied presence, the soil becomes fertile. Without stable soil, even the clearest intentions struggle to survive.

## Sunlight

Sunlight is awareness. What we bring into conscious attention grows. Awareness illuminates the subtle patterns we unconsciously reinforce—such as anxiety, defensiveness, comparison, and habitual urgency. With awareness, these patterns loosen their grip. Sunlight does not force change; it makes choice possible.

## Water

Water is practice. It is the steady nourishment that sustains growth over time. Breathwork, centering, reflection, and micro-practices are small but consistent acts of care. Without practice, insight dries out. With practice, aspiration becomes embodied.

## Life-Force

Life-force is the vitality that animates the inner garden. It is the sense of aliveness, coherence, and flow that arises when mind, heart, and body are aligned. Wisdom traditions describe this vital energy in different ways but point to the same truth: when we are present and grounded, vitality circulates. When life-force is alive, growth accelerates naturally.

## Weeds

Weeds are habitual ego patterns, such as reactivity, avoidance, fear-based defenses, and self-centeredness, that grow when left unattended. They are not enemies; they are signals. Weeds reveal where attention, healing, and compassion are needed. When met consciously, they create space for authenticity and essence to emerge.

Across wisdom traditions, the message is consistent: we do not grow by force; we grow by tending.

When the soil is grounded, the seeds are clear, awareness is steady, practice is consistent, vitality is alive, and ego patterns are met with awareness, leadership becomes an expression of natural growth rather than strain. We do not have to force who we are becoming. We create the conditions through which we can unfold.

## Habits of Essence vs. Habits of Ego

If the inner garden is the landscape of leadership, habits are the daily rhythms that shape it. Habit is how cultivation becomes identity. What we practice repeatedly becomes our way of being, because repetition makes it second nature.

Every leader lives with two sets of habits at once: habits of ego and habits of essence. Both are learned. Both can be unlearned. In each moment, we are strengthening one or the other.

### Habits of Ego: Patterns That Contract Us

Ego habits are not personal flaws; they are survival strategies. They are ways of managing uncertainty, protecting identity, or avoiding discomfort. They once served us. Over time, they harden into patterns that limit presence and distort perception.

These habits show up as contraction in the body and a narrowing of awareness. Before a difficult conversation, we brace. Under pressure, breath shortens, muscles tighten, and attention collapses around control, defense, or urgency. Decisions become reactive rather than responsive.

Ego habits persist not because they are true, but because they are efficient. They have been rehearsed for years. They feel familiar.

Like weeds in a garden, they grow automatically when left unattended. They call for neither shame nor blame—only awareness.

## Habits of Essence: Practices That Expand Us

Habits of essence arise when the nervous system is regulated, and attention is no longer organized around protection. They are felt immediately in the body: breath deepens, tension softens, awareness widens.

We pause before responding. We listen more fully. We return to center when pressure appears. We speak truth without force. We reorient to purpose when doubt or distraction arises.

At first, these habits require intention. With repetition, they become natural. The nervous system learns that presence is safer than reactivity, that openness carries more wisdom than defensiveness, and that groundedness is more trustworthy than pressure. Essence becomes the baseline rather than the exception.

Ego habits tend to be reactive, defensive, controlling, and self-image-driven, while essence habits are responsive, curious, grounded, and aligned.

There comes a subtle moment when something shifts. Instead of tightening, we breathe. Instead of reacting, we pause. Instead of defending, we listen. Instead of collapsing into old narratives, we return to center.

This is the crossover point—when habits of essence begin to activate automatically. It is not willpower; it is rewiring. Cultivation becomes embodied. Leadership becomes an expression of who we are, not a performance we manage.

Consider a leader walking into a meeting where a critical project has slipped again. An ego habit activates instantly. The body tightens. The jaw clenches. The breath shortens. The leader's voice sharpens as questions turn into pressure: "Why wasn't this anticipated?" "How did we miss this—again?" Attention collapses. People begin explaining instead of thinking. The room shifts into self-protection, and useful information goes quiet. Compliance follows, but ownership does not.

An essence habit meets the same moment with steadiness. The delay is still addressed clearly—standards are not lowered—but the body remains grounded. The leader pauses, the breath steadies, and attention stays open before speaking. Instead of pressing for explanations, they ask what is actually constraining progress. As tension softens, the room opens. Hidden risks surface. Accountability and ownership deepen. The team shifts from defending to addressing root causes and solving the problem—not because pressure was removed, but because presence replaced it.

Ego habits do not disappear because we understand them. They soften because something stronger is being practiced. Emotion becomes information, not identity. Tension becomes a signal, not a command. Cultivation is not about perfection. It is about intentional practice.

In the age of artificial intelligence, inner habits are not replaced; they are revealed. AI accelerates habit evolution by making patterns visible that would otherwise remain unconscious. Through data, language analysis, reflection tools, and behavioral tracking, it shortens the feedback loop between action and awareness.[14]

This matters because habit change begins with seeing clearly. AI can highlight patterns of urgency, defensiveness, avoidance, or clarity—without judgment, and at scale.

What AI cannot do is practice on our behalf. It cannot breathe, soften the body, reorient intention, or choose presence over reactivity. Those capacities remain irreducibly human.

Used consciously, AI becomes a mirror that reflects our patterns so they can be cultivated rather than reinforced. Used unconsciously, it simply accelerates whatever habits are already in place. As AI takes on more information processing, leaders are called to take responsibility for what they are reinforcing beneath the surface: the quality of attention they bring, the tone of their responses, and the impact those responses have on others and the systems they shape.

## Energetic Cultivation

Cultivation is not only psychological or behavioral. It is also energetic.

Every thought, emotion, intention, and habit carries an energetic signature that shapes how we feel, how we lead, and how others experience us. Presence is energetic before it is verbal. Stance is energetic before it is visible. Leadership is felt before it is understood.

Most leadership development focuses on what leaders think or do. Yet leadership begins at a more subtle level—long before action or language. When energy is scattered or contracted, people feel it immediately. When it is coherent and grounded, they feel that too. Energy is the silent architecture of leadership.

Across wisdom traditions, human beings have been understood as layered: physical, emotional, mental, energetic, and spiritual. Modern neuroscience increasingly reveals a convergence with this view. Research on nervous system regulation, physiological coherence, and interpersonal attunement suggests that what we call presence is a lived, embodied state that organizes perception, tone, and response before words are formed or actions are taken.[13]

This is why presence cannot be improvised. Under pressure, the body does not rise to intention—it returns to what it has been conditioned to hold. A leader who has cultivated regulation and coherence can stabilize a room without speaking, not through effort, but through the steadiness of their internal state. A leader whose system is fragmented may unsettle others despite insight, skill, or good intent.

Energetic cultivation works at this level. It is the long-term refinement of the subtle forces that shape presence. Through practices of breath, attention, movement, and dedication, leaders train the nervous system to remain grounded and open under pressure. As the inner state becomes regulated, breath deepens, posture settles, and attention steadies. Others feel safer, more relaxed, and more honest—not because of what the leader does, but because of the energy they carry.

Energetic cultivation is not about amplifying intensity. It is about restoring flow.

## Transmutation: Turning Inner States into Strength

As energetic cultivation deepens, transmutation becomes possible. It creates the capacity to remain present with inner experience until its energy reorganizes into clarity and strength.

Transmutation is not suppression or denial. It is the art of staying with what arises without collapsing into it or pushing it away.

Fear can sharpen awareness.

Anger can reveal violated values and boundaries.

Anxiety can heighten perception when allowed to move.

Tension can consolidate into grounded power.

Grief can deepen compassion.

Pressure can crystallize purpose.

Like raw ore refined by heat, emotional charge becomes inner strength through presence.

Transmutation begins in the body. The breath deepens. The jaw releases. The belly softens. The spine lengthens. As the body opens, the nervous system shifts from protection into presence. What once felt overwhelming begins to move. What once felt dense begins to reorganize.

Certain contemplative practices and ancient techniques, often described as technologies for inducing expanded or holotropic states of consciousness, can intentionally loosen habitual patterns of perception, emotion, and identity. These states can reveal layers of clarity and meaning beyond ordinary awareness, not by adding something new, but by temporarily removing the filters through which experience is normally interpreted.

These moments reveal latent capacity. Leaders may glimpse coherence, depth, or presence that lies beyond their habitual operating range. These experiences can be illuminating precisely because they show what becomes possible when conditioned patterns loosen.

Yet insight alone does not transform leadership. Without integration, what is seen remains episodic. Without cultivation, it fades under pressure. Used wisely, such states serve as orientation points rather than destinations—reminders of depth rather than replacements for practice. Cultivation is what makes insight durable. It allows clarity to stabilize, presence to mature, and capacity to become embodied over time.

When a leader cultivates their energy, something subtle but unmistakable shifts. They feel grounded without rigidity, open without exposure, powerful without force. Others breathe easier around them.

Energetic leadership is the natural expression of someone who has learned to stand in their center and meet life with an open, steady heart.

## Cultivating Higher Human Capacities

As energy, presence, and coherence are cultivated, deeper human capacities begin to awaken—capacities that exist within every person but remain dormant when the nervous system is contracted, and attention is absorbed by survival and control.

Across history, these capacities have appeared in mystics, sages, artists, healers, and visionaries. Today, they are increasingly explored through transpersonal psychology, neuroscience, and consciousness research—not as anomalies, but as expressions of latent human potential.

In a world shaped by artificial intelligence, these capacities are no longer optional. AI will surpass humans in speed, memory, and information processing, but it cannot feel, intuit, resonate, or access meaning. The future does not ask leaders to compete with machines; it invites them to cultivate the dimensions of humanness that cannot be automated.

Intuition is an advanced perceptual capacity that integrates subconscious pattern recognition, emotional intelligence, somatic awareness, and sensitivity to subtle relational, emotional, and informational patterns, thus allowing insight to arise as immediate understanding rather than deliberate analysis. As presence deepens and inner noise quiets, intuition becomes a reliable form of guidance, especially in complex situations where data is incomplete and logic alone is insufficient. Leaders who cultivate this capacity sense timing, direction, and coherence without needing control.

As coherence increases, perception refines. Leaders begin to sense the emotional and relational atmosphere of a room without relying solely on words. They notice what is unspoken, detect tension or alignment, and feel resonance or discord, much like a musician hears subtle shifts in tone. This is not mystical; it is attunement. When the mind is quiet and the body is grounded, perception widens, allowing leaders to intervene earlier, navigate conflict more skillfully, and respond to emerging dynamics before they become visible breakdowns.

Creativity flourishes in spaciousness. When ego relaxes and energy flows, imagination becomes receptive rather than forced. Many creators describe insight as something received rather than produced, with ideas arriving whole, images arising fully formed, strategies emerging organically, and solutions revealing themselves when effort gives way to presence. Cultivation does not manufacture creativity; it removes what blocks it. In coherent states, vision clarifies, and creativity becomes a natural byproduct of alignment rather than strain.

Certain contemplative practices and breathwork techniques can reliably induce expanded states of awareness that temporarily reveal dimensions of wholeness beyond ordinary cognition. Stanislav Grof described such experiences as holotropic. These are states that orient us toward wholeness.[15] Their value lies not only in the experience itself, but in the capacities they reveal: clarity of purpose, emotional release, deep insight, and a felt sense of connection beyond egoic identity. Used wisely, these states become part of cultivation, revealing capacities that integration and daily practice gradually stabilize.

These capacities—intuition, subtle perception, creativity, and expanded awareness—mark the next evolution of leadership. As artificial intelligence accelerates cognition, the role of human leadership clarifies. What cannot be automated—presence, discernment, meaning, and wisdom—moves to the center. Cultivation deepens the being, where machines expand the mind

For the first time, humanity has both the freedom and the necessity to develop abilities once associated only with rare individuals. The central question of leadership is no longer only *what can humans know?* But what *can humans become?* Cultivating higher human capacities is not about becoming superhuman; it is about becoming fully human, awakening the deeper architecture of intelligence, perception, and wisdom that has always been part of our design. Through cultivation, leadership becomes not merely a role, but an expression of expanded human potential.

## Tools of Cultivation

Cultivation does not happen by accident. We do not evolve simply through age or experience; we evolve through intentional practice—through tools that refine perception, regulate the nervous system, expand awareness, and reorganize the inner architecture of the self. Tools are not the path; they are gateways into it.

Across cultures and traditions, human beings have always used tools to awaken latent capacities. In an age where artificial intelligence accelerates thought but not awareness, these tools become central—as supports for becoming more present, coherent, and whole.

### Foundational Regulation: Establishing the Ground

All cultivation rests on stability. Foundational practices regulate the nervous system, quiet mental noise, and restore contact with the body and heart. Without this ground, deeper work cannot be integrated.

Practices such as conscious breathing, meditation, somatic presence, and heart-centered reflection create the conditions for clarity and resilience. They are not optional preliminaries; they are the soil in which everything else grows.

### Energetic Vitality: Strengthening the Inner Current

Beyond regulation lies vitality: the life-force that fuels presence, intuition, and creativity. Many traditions have developed ways of refining this inner current through breath, movement, sound, and focused attention.

Music and sound are among the most powerful—and underappreciated—tools of cultivation. Rhythm, melody, and harmonic resonance interact directly with the nervous system, bypassing cognitive filters and organizing inner experience at a pre-verbal level. Used consciously, music can regulate state, release emotional charge, expand perception, and open access to creativity and insight. Across cultures, sound has been used not only for relaxation, but for healing, trance, prayer, and communion—because it entrains coherence.

Unlike conceptual tools, music works through resonance. It does not instruct the mind; it reorganizes the system. When vitality is cultivated through coherent sound, leaders feel grounded yet open, steady yet flexible, powerful without force.

### Insight and Expanded Awareness: Accessing Deeper Intelligence

Certain contemplative and breath-based practices can open access to expanded modes of awareness—states that reveal deeper patterns of meaning, purpose, and connection. These experiences are not only valuable because they are extraordinary, but because they reveal capacities that can later be embodied in ordinary life.

When approached responsibly and with proper support, such tools can soften rigid mental structures, release long-held emotional patterns, and reconnect individuals with a wider sense of self and meaning. They are not the path itself; they illuminate what the path makes possible.

Among these tools, psychedelic-assisted therapy has re-emerged in modern research as a powerful catalyst when used intentionally and ethically.[16] With proper preparation, skilled facilitation, and careful integration, these experiences can temporarily loosen entrenched cognitive and emotional patterns, making insight and perspective more accessible. Their value lies not in intensity, but in what they reveal and make available for sustained cultivation.

## Integration and Shadow Work: Cultivating Wholeness

Cultivation is not only upward; it is also inward. Growth requires integrating the parts of ourselves that were fragmented, suppressed, or exiled in the process of adaptation and survival.

Tools for inner integration, such as parts work, somatic inquiry, trauma-informed awareness, and reflective practices, allow emotional energy to reorganize rather than overwhelm.[17] They transform reactivity into wisdom and restore coherence where inner conflict once lived.

## Using Tools Wisely

Powerful tools require maturity. Intention shapes experience, consistency shapes transformation, and integration determines whether change becomes lasting.

Not all tools are meant to be practiced alone. Some require skilled guidance, ethical boundaries, and careful integration. The aim is not to collect methods, but to commit deeply to the few that genuinely support becoming.

Cultivation is not a performance. It is a devotion to truth, presence, and the fullest expression of our human potential.

## TAKEAWAYS

- Conscious leadership is cultivated, not discovered.

  Insight may open the door, but cultivation is what allows us to walk the path. Who we become is shaped by what we practice repeatedly.

- Cultivation is about coherence, not intensity.

  Growth does not require dramatic breakthroughs. It unfolds through steady returns—to breath, body, awareness, and intention.

- The nervous system is the ground of leadership.

  Without regulation and embodied presence, clarity collapses, and insight cannot integrate. Stability precedes expansion.

- Energy shapes presence before action.

  Leaders transmit coherence—or fragmentation—long before they speak. Cultivating vitality refines how we are felt, not just what we do.

- Expanded awareness reveals deeper intelligence.

  Certain practices open access to intuition, creativity, and meaning beyond ordinary cognition. Their value lies in what becomes embodied afterward.

- Integration matters more than experience.

  Without grounding and integration, insight fades. With maturity and responsibility, it reshapes identity, choice, and presence.

- Cultivation is inseparable from wholeness.

  Inner work, shadow integration, and emotional transmutation transform reactivity into wisdom and restore coherence where fragmentation once lived.

- ✦ In the age of AI, cultivation becomes essential.

  As machines accelerate thinking, leadership shifts toward presence, discernment, compassion, intuition, and coherence, the dimensions of humanness that cannot be automated.

- ✦ Cultivation is a devotion, not a performance.

  The aim is not to master many tools, but to commit deeply to the practices that genuinely support our becoming.

## PRACTICES

Cultivation is not something you add to life; it is how you meet life. These practices are not meant to be completed or mastered. They are invitations, ways of returning, again and again, to the ground from which conscious leadership grows.

### 1. Daily Grounding: Returning to the Body

At least once a day, pause and bring attention fully into the body.

Feel your feet on the ground.

Sense the weight of your body.

Allow the breath to settle naturally, without forcing it.

Notice:

- *Is your system rushed or settled?*
- *Is there tension you can soften without effort?*

This simple return regulates the nervous system and restores coherence. Over time, it becomes the baseline from which you lead rather than an interruption to action.

### 2. Cultivating the Inner Garden

Once a week, reflect quietly on your inner landscape.

Ask yourself:

- *What have I been nourishing lately: presence or reactive urgency?*
- *What habits feel like seeds beginning to grow?*
- *What reactions or patterns feel like weeds asking for attention?*

Do not try to fix anything. Simply notice. Awareness itself begins the work of cultivation.

### 3. Choosing One Anchor Practice

Rather than engaging many practices lightly, choose one primary anchor for a season.

Return to one of the core tools introduced in this chapter—whether from foundational regulation, energetic vitality, expanded awareness, or integration and shadow work. Take a moment to review these practices and notice which one resonates most with you at this point. Choose it and commit to it as your ground.

Commit to returning to this practice consistently—not perfectly, but faithfully. Cultivation deepens through repetition, not variety.

### 4. Integration After Insight

If you engage in practices that open expanded awareness—such as deep breathwork, psychedelic-assisted therapy, or other non-ordinary states—treat integration as the real practice.

In the days and weeks that follow, inquire:

- ✦ *What quality is asking to be embodied now?*
- ✦ *How does this insight want to live in my daily choices?*
- ✦ *What small habit would honor what I saw?*

Insight without integration fades. Integration is what allows experience to become character.

### 5. Noticing the Direction of Becoming

Periodically, either monthly or even quarterly, pause and sense the trajectory of your cultivation.

Reflect:

- *Am I becoming more grounded or more reactive?*
- *More open or more defended?*
- *More coherent or more fragmented?*

Cultivation is not about perfection. It is about direction.

### 6. A Closing Reflection

End your practice, however brief, by remembering this:

You do not force who you are becoming.

You create the conditions in which you can unfold.

Each return to presence, each moment of regulation, each act of awareness is a quiet vote for the leader you are growing into.

# PART II

# Leading With Others

CHAPTER 5

# Conscious Listening

*Listen with the ear of your heart.*

—Rumi

We were born with two ears and one mouth—a quiet invitation from nature to listen more than we speak. And yet, *how often do we truly listen? What is the quality of our listening?*

In many conversations, we are already forming our response before the other person has finished speaking. We listen to confirm what we believe, to agree or disagree, or to find the next opportunity to interject. Much of what passes for listening is actually preparation—attention turned toward what we will say next rather than what is being offered now.

Conscious listening is something far deeper. It is not only about hearing words; it is about receiving. It is an act of presence, openness, and willingness to encounter another person without immediately organizing, correcting, or judging their experience. It includes sensitivity not only to what is spoken, but to what is hesitated, softened, or left unsaid.

Listening is fundamentally receptive. Just as we breathe in to receive fresh air, we listen to receive meaning, perspective, and lived experience. Speaking is an exhale—an expression of thought, intention, and direction. Listening, at its deepest level, is an inhale. It nourishes awareness, widens perception, and allows reality to enter us before we respond to it.

In leadership, the cost of poor listening is subtle but cumulative. Misalignment, disengagement, and erosion of trust rarely begin with open conflict. They begin when people sense they are no longer being received. Conscious listening is therefore not merely a communication skill; it is a stance toward what is actually present. It transforms leadership from managing conversations into participating in meaning-making—where connection, insight, and shared understanding can genuinely emerge.

## How We Commonly Listen

We do not hear reality as it is; we hear it through our conditioning, biases, and past experiences. Our minds filter information constantly, deciding what is relevant and what is not—often without our awareness.

This filtering is not a flaw. It is how the brain manages complexity. While the nervous system processes vast amounts of information every second, only a small fraction reaches conscious awareness.[1] The rest is automatically sorted, categorized, and interpreted. These mental shortcuts allow us to function efficiently—but they also narrow perception.

Over time, these filters reinforce familiar patterns of thinking. We notice what confirms our existing beliefs and overlook what challenges them. We hear certain voices more clearly than others.

Meaning is assigned not only to what is said, but to who is saying it, how it aligns with expectations, and whether it fits the story we already hold.

In leadership, these filters are often strengthened by past success. What has worked before becomes a reference point for what feels trustworthy now. A leader may unconsciously privilege certain perspectives while discounting others; not out of ill will, but out of habit. Concerns raised by familiar "types" are minimized. Ideas from trusted sources are elevated without deeper examination. Blind spots form quietly, reinforced by efficiency and repetition rather than intent.

Beneath these filters lies an even subtler dynamic: we do not only listen through bias—we listen through prediction. Much of what we hear is shaped by what we already expect to hear.[2] The mind anticipates meaning in advance, filling in gaps, resolving ambiguity, and stabilizing reality before it fully arrives. When incoming information matches expectation, listening feels smooth. When it does not, tension arises—not because something is wrong, but because prediction has been disrupted.

Alongside filtering and prediction, another habit shapes how we listen: we listen to respond rather than to receive. Attention shifts from the speaker to the internal narrative—evaluating, preparing, correcting, deciding. What appears as engagement is often anticipation. The conversation advances, but understanding does not deepen.

These patterns are rarely deliberate. They are conditioned responses designed to conserve effort and maintain familiarity. And they shape relationships in subtle ways. When listening is filtered through assumption and oriented toward response, nuance disappears. Perspectives flatten. People begin to sense—often without being able to articulate it—that what they offer may not fully matter.

This is not a failure of character or competence. It is the default mode of habitual listening. And recognizing it is the first step toward listening differently. Conscious listening begins when we notice prediction at work and choose curiosity over certainty, thus allowing reality to reveal itself rather than confirming what we already believe.

In the early days, David had relied on Maya.

She was one of the few people on his executive team who would challenge him openly. In meetings, she asked uncomfortable questions, pushed back on assumptions, and slowed conversations that were moving too fast. At times, her perspective complicated things—but it also sharpened them. David didn't always agree with her, but he trusted her intelligence and her willingness to speak up.

Over time, that changed. Maya was still present, still prepared, still reliable. But the edge in her voice softened. The questions grew fewer. When disagreements surfaced, she deferred more quickly. In meetings where she once leaned forward, she now leaned back.

At first, David welcomed the shift. There was less friction. Decisions moved faster. Alignment seemed easier. And yet, something felt off.

What unsettled him wasn't anything she said; it was what she no longer said. The absence of her perspective left conversations flatter, thinner. David found himself wondering when it had happened, when her engagement had quietly turned into distance.

The next one-on-one followed a familiar pattern. David laid out priorities, shared updates, and asked for her thoughts. Maya listened attentively and responded politely.

"It all sounds good," she said. "I don't really have anything to add."

David felt a flicker of irritation. He had asked for her perspective. He missed the Maya who would slow him down, challenge him, make him think. Instead, he was met with what felt like withdrawal disguised as agreement.

As he began to respond, something caught his attention—not in her words, but in himself. A tightness in his chest. A subtle urge to move the conversation forward. To fill the space. To stay in control.

He paused.

For the first time, David noticed how he had been listening—not to understand Maya, but to manage the conversation. To keep things efficient. To avoid the discomfort that often followed her earlier pushback. He realized that each time she had raised concerns in the past, he had acknowledged them—then continued on unchanged. Her resistance hadn't been met with curiosity; it had been met with momentum.

He softened his posture and let the silence linger.

After a moment, he said quietly, "I might be missing something. And I want to check—how is this actually landing for you?"

Maya looked down. Then back up. Her voice was steady, but something underneath it shifted.

"I didn't think it mattered anymore," she said. "I used to push back because I cared. But after a while, it felt like my concerns were heard—and then bypassed. It just seemed easier to stop bringing them up."

The words landed heavily.

David resisted the urge to explain himself. Or to defend his intentions. Or to reassure her too quickly. He stayed present, letting her words register fully.

"I didn't realize that's how it felt," he said. "But I'm really glad you said it."

Maya exhaled. Her shoulders dropped slightly.

"I want to be engaged," she said. "I just didn't know if there was space for it anymore."

In that moment, nothing was resolved. No decisions were revisited. No commitments were renegotiated. But something essential returned.

Connection.

David listened differently for the rest of the conversation—not searching for solutions but making room for what had been unsaid. Maya spoke more freely. Not everything she shared was comfortable to hear. But it was real.

The withdrawal hadn't been a lack of engagement. It had been a response to not being fully heard.

By listening without an agenda, David hadn't fixed the situation. He had reopened the relationship.

And that was enough to begin again. Conscious listening did not change the agenda. It changed the field in which the agenda lived.

## Listening Beneath the Words

Much of what shapes connection in leadership conversations is never spoken.

Words carry meaning, but they represent only one layer of communication. Tone, pacing, posture, pauses, and emotional charge often convey more than content alone[2] Research in communication and neuroscience suggests that non-verbal and para-verbal cues are registered by the nervous system before language is consciously processed.[3] Long before we analyze what is being said, we sense how it is being said—and the internal state from which it arises.

Conscious listening attunes to this deeper layer. It listens not only for information, but for shifts in presence. A quick agreement may conceal hesitation. Politeness may mask frustration. Withdrawal may appear as cooperation. When leaders attend only to words, these signals are easily missed—and relationships quietly drift out of alignment.

Psychologist Carl Rogers observed that deep listening involves more than hearing content. It requires attunement to emotional undercurrents and the capacity to remain present without immediate evaluation, correction, or agenda. When people feel this quality of attention, they become more willing to speak honestly and explore what they are actually experiencing—not just what feels safe to say.[4]

This form of listening depends on a relaxed, open awareness rather than a narrow focus. In martial arts traditions such as Aikido and Tai Chi, practitioners cultivate a soft gaze—a wide, unfixed field of perception that allows subtle movement and intention to be sensed without strain. Conscious listening operates in a similar way. Instead of fixating on words alone, the listener softens attention and takes in the whole relational field.

Silence plays a critical role here. Pauses are not empty space; they often hold uncertainty, emotion, or insight still forming. When leaders rush to fill the silence, they may interrupt what is trying to emerge. When they remain present within it, deeper truth has room to surface.

Listening beneath the words requires a different kind of attention. Rather than analyzing or interrogating, it involves witnessing—the capacity to remain open to what is unfolding without immediately categorizing, fixing, or responding. In that openness, what was previously hidden often becomes visible, and what felt disconnected can begin to reconnect.

## Listening to Self While Listening to Others

Conscious listening includes awareness of one's inner experience. Listening always unfolds through two channels at once: attention directed outward toward the other person, and attention directed inward toward our own inner movements. When either channel collapses, listening loses depth. When both remain open, presence stabilizes.

As we listen to others, thoughts arise. Judgments form. Emotions surface. There may be an impulse to interrupt, to clarify, to correct, or to steer the conversation toward resolution. These reactions are not signs of poor listening; they are part of being human. The challenge is not that they occur, but that they often operate unnoticed.

Listening to self while listening to others means becoming aware of internal movements—senses and thoughts—without acting them out. It is the capacity to notice tension, defensiveness, impatience, or urgency as they arise, in the body as much as in the mind, without allowing them to narrow attention or diminish presence. This awareness creates a space between stimulus and response. In that space, choice becomes possible.

When judgment takes hold too quickly, curiosity collapses, and with it, the possibility of learning something new.

Without this internal awareness, listening easily collapses into self-reference. The conversation becomes filtered through personal reactions, unresolved emotions, or the need to maintain control. Attention turns inward in a contracted way, narrowing perception rather than expanding it. What might have been a moment of connection becomes a subtle struggle for position, certainty, or relief from discomfort.

With awareness, something different happens. The leader remains present even as reactions move through. Thoughts are noticed without being believed. Emotions are felt without being projected. Listening becomes steadier, less reactive, and more spacious.

This does not mean withholding truth or suppressing response. It means allowing inner experience to settle enough before speaking. When leaders listen with this quality of self-awareness, their responses arise from clarity rather than reflex. Conversations slow down. Understanding deepens. And trust is strengthened—not because everything is said perfectly, but because presence is maintained.

## Listening as Relational Leadership

Leaders do not only listen to individuals. They listen to relationships.

Every organization is held together not just by structure and strategy, but also by the quality of the connections between people. Listening shapes that quality over time. It signals what matters, whose voices count, and whether it is safe to speak openly. Long before culture is articulated, it is sensed through how leaders listen.

Relational breakdown rarely begins with open conflict. More often, it begins with subtle disengagement. People speak less. They offer fewer perspectives. They stop challenging assumptions. On the surface, things may appear smoother. Beneath it, the relational fabric begins to erode.

The way a leader listens in moments of tension, uncertainty, or disagreement has a disproportionate impact. When listening is rushed, selective, or defensive, people adapt by withdrawing. When listening is present and receptive, people remain engaged—even when conversations are difficult.

Listening as relational leadership does not mean agreeing, accommodating, or avoiding hard decisions. It means recognizing that how decisions are reached shapes the relationship long after the decision itself is made. People can accept outcomes they disagree with when they feel genuinely heard. They disengage when they do not.

Over time, listening becomes self-reinforcing. Leaders who listen deeply invite honesty, initiative, and shared responsibility. Leaders who listen narrowly—often without realizing it—train people to withhold, comply, or disengage. In this way, listening quietly shapes performance, trust, and collective intelligence.

Practiced consistently, conscious listening becomes a stabilizing force within relationships. It creates coherence without control and alignment without coercion. Leadership shifts from managing people to holding the relational field, where clarity, accountability, and connection can coexist.

## Listening as Creative Collaboration

When listening is free of agenda, something unexpected becomes possible.

In many leadership conversations, outcomes are predetermined. Positions are formed in advance, and listening becomes a means of persuasion, validation, or alignment. Creative collaboration, however, requires a different posture. It begins when leaders are willing to listen without knowing exactly where the conversation will lead.

This quality of listening creates space for emergence. Ideas surface that no one arrived with. Insights arise that belong not to any individual, but to the shared field of attention. What emerges is often more nuanced, more integrated, and more innovative than what any one person could have produced alone.

At this level, listening does more than generate ideas; it transmutes what enters the conversation. Partial perspectives soften. Emotional charge reorganizes. Tension becomes information rather than obstacle. What might have appeared as conflict, resistance, or disagreement is gradually transformed into clarity, coherence, or shared direction—not by force, but by sustained presence.

Creative collaboration depends less on brilliance than on receptivity. When leaders listen deeply, they loosen the impulse to dominate, defend, or control the conversation. They allow perspectives to interact, tensions to be held, and meaning to form over time. In this environment, disagreement becomes generative rather than divisive. It becomes something not to eliminate, but something to work with.

Listening in this way also transforms the experience of contribution. People feel invited into creation rather than evaluated for correctness. They take greater ownership of ideas because they have participated in their emergence. Collaboration becomes an act of shared authorship rather than a negotiated compromise.

This does not mean deferring decisions indefinitely or seeking consensus at the expense of clarity. Leadership still requires judgment, timing, and the willingness to decide. Conscious listening does not replace authority—it informs it. Most people do not need every decision to go their way; they need to feel genuinely heard and meaningfully considered. When leaders listen deeply before acting, decisions are often made with greater confidence and far less resistance, because the relational field has already been engaged.

At this level, listening is no longer passive. It becomes a creative act of trust, a trust that intelligence is distributed, that insight can emerge through relationship, and that leadership does not require having the answer in advance. By listening openly, leaders do not surrender authority; they refine it, thereby creating the conditions in which disagreement, challenge, and diverse perspectives can interact until a form of intelligence emerges that no single person could have produced alone.

## TAKEAWAYS

- Conscious listening is not just a communication skill; it is a relational expression of conscious stance, grounded in receptivity and presence.
- Most listening is shaped by filters—identity, urgency, assumptions, and the impulse to respond—which quietly narrow understanding.
- What disrupts connection is often not what is said, but what goes unnoticed: tone, hesitation, withdrawal, and silence.
- Deep listening requires awareness of one's own internal reactions without acting them out. This creates space for choice rather than reflex.
- Listening shapes relationships over time. How leaders listen determines whether people engage, comply, or withdraw.
- Creative collaboration emerges when listening is free of agenda and open to what wants to arise, not just what was planned.
- Decisive leadership does not require consensus. Most people do not need their preferred outcome. They need to feel heard and considered.
- When leaders listen deeply before acting, decisions are clearer, and execution moves faster because people feel heard even when outcomes differ.

## PRACTICES

Conscious listening is a practice you return to. Each conversation offers another opportunity to listen more fully—to others, to yourself, and to what is emerging between you. The practices that follow are not meant to be mastered but revisited over time. Let them shape how you show up, rather than how you perform.

### 1. The Pause Before Response

In conversations that matter, notice the moment just before you speak. That instant often carries impulse: agreement, correction, explanation, or defense.

Practice allowing a brief pause before responding, not to calculate a better answer, but to notice what is arising in you. Sense the body. Notice any tightening, urgency, or emotional charge. Let the reaction settle before you speak.

This pause does not slow leadership; it clarifies it. Over time, it trains the capacity to respond from presence rather than reflex.

### 2. Listening Without Agenda

Choose one conversation each day, whether brief or substantial, where you intentionally release the need to steer, fix, or influence the outcome.

Listen without preparing a response. Let the other person finish fully. Attend not only to their words, but to tone, pacing, and moments of hesitation. Notice how quickly the mind wants to intervene and gently return attention to receiving.

This practice develops receptivity, which is the foundation of conscious listening, and reveals how often listening is shaped by hidden agendas.

**3. Noticing Withdrawal**

Pay attention to moments when engagement subtly fades, whether through shorter answers, reduced eye contact, polite agreement, or emotional distance.

Instead of moving past these moments, acknowledge them with curiosity. A simple observation such as, *"Something feels different right now—am I sensing that correctly?"* can reopen connection.

This practice strengthens sensitivity to what is unspoken and builds trust without confrontation.

**4. Listening to Self in Real Time**

During challenging conversations, allow part of your attention to remain with your inner experience. Notice judgments, emotional reactions, or assumptions as they arise.

Rather than suppressing these experiences, observe them without acting on them immediately. You may gently ask yourself: *What reaction is moving through me right now?* Notice where it is felt in the body and how it is shaping your attention.

Let this noticing create awareness, not analysis. Allow the reaction to pass before responding. Over time, this practice strengthens the capacity to remain present under pressure and prevents listening from collapsing into self-reference.

### 5. Closing the Loop

After making a decision—especially one that may disappoint others—take a moment to acknowledge what was heard.

You might say, "I want you to know that your concerns were considered, even though the decision went another way." This signals respect and recognition without weakening authority.

Over time, this practice reinforces the distinction between being heard and getting one's way, and sustains engagement even in disagreement.

CHAPTER 6

# Conscious Relating

*Out beyond ideas of wrongdoing and rightdoing,*
*there is a field. I'll meet you there.*
—Rumi

Leadership is a relational act.

No matter how skilled, visionary, or capable we become, our true impact is measured in the quality of our connection with ourselves, with others, and with the larger field we serve. Conscious relating is how leaders transform relationships into spaces of trust, creativity, and shared possibility.

To relate consciously is to meet others from essence rather than ego.

It is to bring presence instead of performance, curiosity instead of judgment, and openness instead of protection. Every interaction creates a field—an emotional and energetic atmosphere that shapes how people feel, think, communicate, and collaborate. When leaders cultivate relational awareness, this field becomes an amplifier of clarity, safety, and inspiration.

At the heart of conscious relating lies a profound truth: no two people experience reality in the same way.

We each live in our own inner world shaped by history, emotional conditioning, belief, and perception. When leaders understand this, blame softens, judgment dissolves, and compassion becomes possible. Perspective-shifting becomes a superpower. Conversations become more honest. Teams become more resilient. Connection becomes a gateway to collective intelligence.

Relating consciously is not about being agreeable or "nice." It is about being real—grounded, attuned, and willing to see and be seen. It invites leaders to communicate authentically, to listen generously, to navigate conflict through understanding rather than force, and to build agreements instead of relying on hidden expectations.

In a world increasingly shaped by screens, disembodied communication, and algorithmic interactions, conscious relating becomes a radical act of leadership.

In an age where artificial intelligence increasingly mediates communication, the quality of human relating matters more. Speed, efficiency, and optimization can be automated; mutual understanding cannot. Without conscious relating, technology amplifies misunderstanding. With it, difference becomes a source of coherence rather than division.

Conscious relating is the art of elevating human connection. It is how leaders create belonging, coherence, and shared purpose. It is how we bring joy and beauty into our relationships. It is how we remember our shared humanity, and how we lead from it.

## The Essence of Conscious Relating

Conscious relating begins with a simple yet transformative recognition: every relationship is a living field. Whenever two people meet, whether in conversation, in conflict, in silence, or in collaboration, what becomes possible between them is shaped by the quality of presence they bring.

To relate consciously is to take responsibility for the field you create. It is the practice of meeting others from essence rather than ego—not through performance or strategy, but through presence, authenticity, and attunement. Conscious relating asks us to see the human, not the role; the inner world, not the surface behavior. When we do, the relationship becomes more honest, more spacious, and more capable of transformation.

At its core, conscious relating rests on three foundational capacities:

### Presence

Being fully here—not distracted, not preparing your next point, not tightening in anticipation. Presence is the anchor that allows connection to deepen. When a leader is present, others feel seen in ways that are rare and unforgettable.

### Honoring the Whole Person

Every person carries history, hopes, wounds, gifts, fears, and potentials. Conscious relating is the decision to meet others as whole beings rather than as tools, obstacles, or projections. This simple shift dissolves relational tension and invites authentic collaboration.

## Seeing and Being Seen

Human beings long to be understood. When we are seen accurately and compassionately, something in us relaxes. We stop performing and start relating. Conscious leaders develop the ability to see others clearly while also allowing themselves to be seen—not in their polished image, but in their humanity.

When these capacities converge, relating becomes more than communication. It becomes coherence, a state in which two people feel aligned, connected, and capable of shared insight.

In this state, conversations become more honest, differences become bridges instead of barriers, creativity emerges naturally, and trust deepens without being forced.

Conscious relating is about consistent awareness—the willingness to meet another person from your center, with curiosity rather than judgment, and with openness rather than protection.

This is the foundation upon which all other relational skills are built, and it prepares us for the next essential insight: No two people see the world the same way, and understanding this truth changes everything about how we relate.

## Separate Realities

One of the greatest shifts a leader can make is realizing that no two people live in the same reality. We assume we are experiencing "the world," but in truth, we are each experiencing **our world**—a private, inner landscape shaped by memory, emotional conditioning, culture, belief, temperament, nervous system patterns, and personal history.

Two people can sit in the same meeting and walk away with entirely different interpretations. Not because one is right and the other is wrong, but because they were never perceiving the same experience to begin with. This is the heart of conscious relating: we are all living inside different worlds.

This understanding reshapes how leaders interpret behavior. Instead of assuming intent or taking reactions personally, we begin to recognize that people respond from the reality they inhabit, not from ours. Conflicts become expressions of differing interpretations rather than battles of right and wrong. Tension becomes information. And differences become invitations to explore rather than threats to defend against.

This shift softens judgment and expands possibility. When we stop insisting that others see what we see, we create space for discovery, collaboration, and shared meaning to emerge.

Seeing separate realities does not mean we agree with someone's perspective. It means we recognize that their perspective is real to them. It honors the dignity of their experience without collapsing into it.

From this awareness, leaders gain a remarkable capacity: *perspective-shifting*. This is the ability to step out of one's own world and explore another's without losing oneself. This is one of the most powerful relational skills a leader can cultivate. It transforms conflict, deepens trust, and opens pathways to co-creation that are impossible when leaders are trapped inside their own viewpoint.

Separate realities also reveal why misunderstandings are inevitable. Every relationship is a merging of two invisible worlds, and no one sees the world "as it is." We see it through filters, through meaning-making systems that operate beneath consciousness.

When leaders recognize this, they stop fighting over interpretations and begin exploring them. They stop defending their position and begin discovering the underlying worldview. They stop trying to win and begin trying to understand.

Separate realities do not divide us. Misunderstanding divides us. Ego divides us. The assumption that our view is the only view divides us.

But when we honor separate realities, we create the conditions for connection: openness, humility, and the willingness to learn from one another's inner world.

Conscious relating begins with presence, but it deepens through this understanding. For only when we acknowledge that each person is living in a different reality can we begin to relate in ways that are generous, flexible, and truly human.

The moment we stop insisting on a single shared reality is the moment we open the door to true collaboration, psychological safety, and relational transformation.

## Relational Mindfulness and Attunement

Conscious relating begins with the capacity to remain awake while in connection. Most people lose presence when interacting with others, either by collapsing into the other person's emotions or disconnecting to protect themselves. Relational mindfulness is the practice of staying centered, embodied, and aware in the midst of relationship. It is mindfulness with another person, not apart from them.

Through relational mindfulness, leaders learn to sense three dimensions at once: what is happening in themselves, what is happening in the other person, and what is happening *between* them. This "between"—the relational field—is often called the *we-space*. It is a living, energetic, and emotional space shaped by the presence, intention, nervous system, and awareness of both people. When two individuals meet with openness and attention, the we-space becomes a source of intelligence and insight that neither person can access alone.

Attunement deepens this ability. It is the skill of feeling another person's world without losing your own center.[6] It is the ability to sense subtle shifts in tone, breath, facial expression, and energy, recognizing what is unspoken yet deeply present. When leaders attune consciously, others feel met, understood, and emotionally accompanied rather than analyzed or judged.

Neuroscience confirms that human nervous systems constantly influence one another.[7] Because nervous systems co-regulate, how a leader shows up shapes not just the tone of the room, but what becomes possible between people.

Relational mindfulness also means staying connected without merging. Leaders often fall into one of two extremes: taking on the emotions of others as their own or withdrawing to avoid discomfort. Conscious relating finds the middle way. It becomes an open heart with clear boundaries. This allows authenticity to emerge on both sides. When the leader remains centered while staying connected, the relationship becomes a space where truth can surface safely.

In this space, listening expands beyond words. Leaders begin perceiving meaning through silence, resonance, breath, and the subtle emotional contours of the moment. They sense misalignment even when speech is polished, sincerity even when confidence wavers, and possibility even in moments of tension. The body becomes a sensitive instrument of relational intelligence.

When relational mindfulness and attunement co-exist, relationships become transformational rather than transactional. People feel seen not only for their roles, but for their inner experience. Conversations move with more depth and clarity. Conflicts soften because both people can sense the humanity of the other. Trust grows naturally. Creativity emerges more easily. The we-space becomes a living field of insight, empathy, and shared intelligence.

This is the essence of conscious relating: staying fully present with another human being while rooted in your own center, creating a relational space where both people can bring their best, most authentic selves forward. It is leadership expressed as connection—not through control, performance, or persuasion, but through presence.

## Authentic Communication

Communication is one of the most misunderstood elements of leadership.

Most people assume communication is about words—choosing the right phrasing, structuring the right message, and presenting information clearly. But in conscious leadership, communication is not a performance. It is an energetic and relational transmission.

Authentic communication begins long before words are spoken. It arises from presence, alignment, and the willingness to speak truth without using truth as a weapon. It is the outward expression of inner clarity. To communicate consciously is to let essence speak rather than ego.

Ego communicates to protect. To defend, to justify, to control outcomes, or to maintain an image.

Essence communicates to connect. To reveal truth without force, to honor the other, and to strengthen the relational field rather than fracture it.

When ego speaks, conversations become guarded. When essence speaks, conversations become transformative.

Many leaders equate authenticity with bluntness or emotional dumping: "I'm just being honest." But truth spoken without awareness becomes aggression. It collapses connection rather than deepening it.

Authentic communication is truth delivered with presence. It holds three commitments simultaneously:

1. **Truth**—what is real
2. **Connection**—preserving the relationship
3. **Impact**—speaking in a way that the other can receive

Truth without attunement is violence. Attunement without truth is avoidance. Conscious communication integrates both.

When a leader speaks from essence, their words land differently. They carry clarity without sharpness, firmness without contraction, and honesty without harm. The listener's nervous system relaxes because the delivery contains no hidden agenda.

Before a single word is spoken, the body already communicates intention. This is why leaders must begin with a simple inner question: *"What is the intention behind what I'm about to say?"*

If the intention is to win, prove, defend, or discharge pressure, the impact will likely be contraction. If the intention is alignment, clarity, or connection, the impact becomes spacious, grounded, and constructive.

Intention is the silent architecture beneath every conversation. It determines whether your words create openness or resistance, healing or harm, alignment or fragmentation.

When intention is clean, communication becomes clean.

## Communicating Impact, Not Just Intent

Most relational breakdowns arise not from harm, but from misunderstanding.

Leaders often defend their actions with: "That wasn't my intention."

But conscious leaders understand a deeper truth: You are responsible not only for your intention, but for your impact. Impact is how your words, tone, and presence land in another person's nervous system.

Two things can be true at once:

- Your intention was positive.
- Your impact triggered contraction.

Conscious communication acknowledges both. Instead of arguing about intention, the leader becomes curious about impact:

- *How did what I said land for you?*
- *What impact did that have?*
- *What did you hear me say?*

This transforms communication from self-defense into relational awareness.

Authentic communication is incomplete without listening. In fact, listening is half of speaking because true communication is not a delivery; it is a co-creation.

Speaking from essence requires slowing down enough to feel the other, adjusting your expression to what the moment calls for, and recognizing when silence carries more power than words.

When leaders speak *and* listen from essence, communication becomes fluid rather than forceful. The relational field becomes intelligent, guiding the conversation forward.

At its highest level, authentic communication becomes a creative act—a moment where truth emerges from the shared field rather than from either person alone.

This is not debate. It is not negotiation. It is not performance. It is two or more human beings entering a space of mutual respect, curiosity, and presence, and allowing something new to be born in the space between them. This is how conscious leaders transform communication into collaboration, and conversation into evolution.

## Leading by Agreement, Not Expectation

Most relational breakdowns—in teams, partnerships, families, and organizations— do not come from bad intentions. They come from unspoken expectations.[8]

Expectations live in the mind. They are invisible, assumed, and often unconscious. We rarely articulate them, yet we react as if others should already know them.

The problem is simple and universal: No one else lives in our reality. What feels obvious to us may be completely invisible to another.

When expectations are not met, disappointment arises. Disappointment becomes frustration. Frustration becomes blame. Blame becomes a relational fracture.

Leaders who rely on expectations inevitably create confusion, resentment, and misalignment—not because their expectations are unreasonable, but because they are unspoken.

Agreements are different. Agreements are conscious, mutual, explicit, and co-created. They bring clarity where the ego prefers assumption. They bring alignment where habit produces guessing. They bring trust where ambiguity breeds tension.

An agreement is not a demand and not a compromise. It is a shared commitment created by both people with equal ownership. It clarifies not only *what* we intend to do, but *how* we intend to be with each other while doing it.

Expectations operate from hierarchy. Agreements operate in partnership.

Expectations leave others guessing. Agreements create shared understanding.

Expectations are static. Agreements are living. They can be revisited, refined, and renegotiated.

In conscious leadership, agreements become the architecture of relational trust. They remove unnecessary emotional friction in collaboration. They transform accountability from obligation into ownership. When agreements are clear, conversations become simpler, conflict becomes more constructive, and responsibility becomes shared rather than imposed. Most importantly, agreements honor the humanity and autonomy of everyone involved.

Instead of assuming understanding, we create it. Instead of blaming after the fact, we align before we begin. Instead of reacting to disappointment, we design for success.

A conscious leader moves from expectation to agreement because they understand that clarity supports trust, and shared clarity enables collaboration.

Leading means co-creating the conditions in which each person knows how to succeed and uphold the integrity of the relationship. When agreements are clear, people feel respected, empowered, and trusted—and they rise to meet that trust.

When expectations are replaced with agreements, relationships become stronger, teams become more aligned, communication becomes clearer, accountability strengthens, and cultures become more grounded in mutual respect.

Agreements are relational commitments. They are the way conscious leaders honor the dignity of others, navigate conflict constructively, and create clarity that supports growth, connection, and shared success.

## Collaboration and Co-Creation

True collaboration emerges only when people feel safe enough to bring their full intelligence, creativity, and perspective into the room. It is not the product of structure alone; it is the fruit of relationship. At its deepest level, collaboration is not simply working together; it is *creating together.*

Most teams do not fail because they lack skills or resources. They fail because they cannot access the collective intelligence that arises only when trust, presence, and relational coherence are strong.

This is where *creative collaboration* begins; in the shift from exchanging ideas to allowing something new, surprising, and meaningful to emerge through the relational field. Creative collaboration is the natural expression of connection grounded in presence.

Co-creation is the next evolution of collaboration. It moves beyond dividing tasks, sharing responsibilities, or coordinating efforts. It is the art of allowing something none of us could have created alone to arise through the space between us.

Ego cannot participate in creative collaboration; it competes, protects, dominates, or withdraws. Essence collaborates easily; it listens, attunes, invites, and builds on what is offered.

When leaders cultivate conscious relating, several shifts naturally occur: People speak more freely. They feel seen, valued, and safe enough to offer emerging, intuitive, or experimental ideas.

Diverse perspectives become assets. Instead of competing viewpoints, the team begins to sense the larger intelligence that holds all perspectives as pieces of a wider truth.

Conflict becomes creative tension. Rather than turning personal, it becomes a dynamic force that can spark insight and innovation.

Responsibility becomes shared. Teams shift from "my idea" or "your project" to "our work," where ownership is distributed and aligned.

When leaders bring presence, attunement, and openness into collaboration, the team's relational field becomes alive. People start to *think together, sense together,* and *imagine together.* The group becomes more intelligent than the sum of its parts.

This is co-creation—a state in which ideas arise not from individuals, but through the synergy created by collective presence.

In this space, creative collaboration becomes natural rather than forced. Innovation flows more easily. Solutions emerge that may seem obvious in hindsight yet remain out of reach through analysis alone.

Creative collaboration requires humility—not the absence of expertise, but the willingness to let the best idea win, regardless of its source. It requires listening not to reply, but to build on what is being said. It requires the courage to soften control in service of something larger, wiser, and more impactful than any one mind.

Leaders who cultivate creative collaboration do more than produce better results. They create cultures where people feel alive, engaged, and connected to something meaningful. They foster a sense of *we* that transcends ego and fuels collective purpose.

Collaboration is the beginning. Creative collaboration is the living expression. Co-creation is the flowering.

It is how leaders unlock collective intelligence and transform groups into living systems capable of extraordinary creation.

## Heart-Centered Relating

Human beings do not connect through intellect alone. We connect through the heart.

The heart is the center of warmth, empathy, intuition, and resonance. When the heart is open, relationships deepen. When it is guarded, communication becomes mechanical, and connection collapses into transaction.

Heart-centered relating is not sentimental or soft. It is the courageous practice of meeting others with openness rather than defensiveness, presence rather than pretense, and sincerity rather than performance. It is the stance of a leader who is willing to feel and to let others be felt.

Modern research affirms what ancient traditions have always known: the heart carries its own intelligence.

Research on heart rate variability (HRV) and vagal regulation suggests that when the autonomic nervous system is more regulated, stress reactivity decreases and social engagement becomes easier.[7] People feel safer around a coherent heart. They also feel seen.

Wisdom traditions have long made the heart central to conscious relating:

- ✦ In Sufi practice, the heart is the mirror of the soul—polished through remembrance, devotion, and presence so that it reflects truth without distortion.

- In Yogic philosophy, the *anahata* chakra represents the unstruck sound—the capacity for love, compassion, and connection that exists beneath personality and fear.
- In Christian mysticism, the heart is the seat of divine union—where separation dissolves, and unity becomes felt, not conceptual.
- In indigenous traditions, the heart is a gateway to relational wisdom—guiding decisions that honor both the individual and the whole.

Across cultures, the message is consistent: The heart is how we recognize ourselves in one another.

Heart-centered relating is also deeply supported by modern psychology. George Pransky describes one of the most transformative relational shifts as *a change of heart*—the moment when our innate goodwill naturally returns.[18] Something softens inside us. Tension releases. We stop seeing the other person as a problem, an adversary, or an obstacle. Goodwill is not a technique; it is a shift in consciousness. When it arises, walls fall, misunderstanding dissolves, and collaboration reopens. A leader approaching others with goodwill does not need perfect language. Their presence communicates safety. Their warmth opens space. Their heart does the work that the mind cannot do alone.

In leadership, heart-centered relating means leading from relational truth rather than egoic performance. It means allowing warmth to coexist with clarity, compassion with discernment, and empathy with boundaries. A heart-centered leader does not lose themselves in others; they simply meet others without closing.

This heart-based openness creates the doorway to unity—the recognition that beneath our separate realities, we share the same human longing: to be seen, to be valued, to belong, and to contribute to something meaningful. This sense of unity is not conceptual; it is felt. When two people are attuned, a *we-space* emerges: a relational field where each person feels more whole, more grounded, and more connected than they could alone. This we-space is the birthplace of community. It is where belonging arises, not from agreement or similarity, but from shared presence.

A heart-centered presence has a noticeable impact on teams: people speak more honestly, take risks more freely, and engage with one another more generously. Conflict softens. Creativity expands. Silos dissolve. The emotional climate becomes more coherent, and the relational field more trustworthy.

Heart-centered relating also allows leaders to hold paradox: firmness without harshness, vulnerability without collapse, authority without domination, and love without sentimentality. It reflects a deeper level of maturity.

Heart-centered relating is how leaders cultivate belonging—through presence. People don't feel they belong because they are included in meetings or copied on documents. They feel they belong when their being is welcomed, when their voice matters, and when their presence is felt as part of a larger whole. This is leadership as the creation of unity: turning individuals into a community and relationships into a living system capable of trust, resilience, and shared purpose.

When leaders relate from the heart, they elevate the relational field from a zone of transaction to a field of transformation. They create spaces where people feel human again: connected, inspired, and part of a larger purpose.

Heart-centered relating is a way of being—a conscious choice to bring warmth, presence, generosity, and humility into every interaction. It is one of the deepest sources of joy and beauty in leadership.

## The Crisis of Disconnection

We live in a time of unprecedented technological connection and unprecedented human disconnection.

People are surrounded by messages yet starving for meaning. They are constantly interacting yet rarely feeling met. Attention is fragmented, presence is diluted, and intimacy—emotional, relational, and communal—is becoming a lost art.

Screens have replaced faces. Text has replaced tone. Efficiency has replaced presence. And a generation is growing up more fluent in digital expression than human vulnerability.

This is the paradox of modern life: We are more connected than ever, and yet more alone than ever.

Social scientists call it the *loneliness epidemic.* Psychologists see rising anxiety, emotional dysregulation, and relational fragility. Leaders feel teams becoming more cautious, less expressive, and more easily overwhelmed. Humans are losing the skills of attunement, conversation, conflict resolution, and embodiment—but these are the very capacities leadership depends on.

Technology has reshaped the relational landscape in ways we are only beginning to understand. Virtual communication flattens the subtle cues through which emotion is felt and understood. Constant notifications keep the nervous system in a state of low-level stress. Algorithms reinforce worldview bubbles, while social media trains the brain for comparison rather than connection. And while remote work offers convenience, it often erodes the subtle signals through which trust is built.

In this environment, conscious relating becomes not only important but essential. It is what brings humanity back into the spaces where it quietly disappeared.

As artificial intelligence accelerates communication and decision-making, the quality of human relating matters more than ever. AI will match or exceed humans in cognition, but it cannot participate in the shared field where trust, repair, and mutual understanding are formed.

AI can generate language, but not presence. It can simulate warmth but not feel it. It can predict emotion but not resonate with it. The danger is not that AI will replace human connection, but that humans will forget how to relate.

When leaders rely too heavily on technology to mediate communication, the relational capacities that make leadership human—empathy, listening, attunement, curiosity—begin to weaken. Without conscious cultivation, these capacities atrophy.

The leaders of the future will not distinguish themselves by knowing more or thinking faster. Machines will handle that. They will distinguish themselves by their ability to cultivate trust, resolve conflict through understanding, create unity out of difference, and bring coherence to complex human systems. This is the relational artistry no machine can replicate.

Concepts become real when we witness them in action. Conscious relating is not an abstract ideal; it is a lived experience that can transform a team, a relationship, or an entire culture in a single moment of presence.

The team had been stuck for months. A product launch was slipping, tensions were rising, and meetings had turned into subtle battles: polite on the surface, tight underneath. People spoke in guarded phrases. Some disengaged. Others dominated. Everyone blamed someone else for the delay, either silently or directly.

The leader, Maya, was exhausted from trying to push the team back into alignment. She increased meetings. She clarified roles. She set tighter deadlines. Nothing worked.

One Thursday morning, after yet another tense review meeting, she paused and realized: "We're not misaligned on strategy. We're disconnected as human beings."

Something in her softened. She could feel her own urgency and frustration, and she could sense the same urgency mirrored in everyone else. Rather than scheduling another problem-solving session, she called the team together for a completely different kind of meeting.

When everyone arrived, she began with slow breath. Just a few seconds of silence—and the whole room shifted. Then she said:

"I want to understand each of your realities. Not your tasks. Not your updates. Your world."

The room went still. No one had ever asked this.

One by one, people shared what was actually happening beneath the surface:

- A designer felt unheard and had stopped speaking up.
- An engineer was overwhelmed and embarrassed to admit he was behind.
- A product manager felt blamed for everything.
- A new team member didn't feel safe enough to challenge decisions.

- Several admitted they didn't actually agree on the expectations they thought were "clear."

As each person spoke, Maya listened—not to fix, but to feel. She mirrored the emotions she saw. She asked curious questions. She acknowledged everyone's reality without judgment.

By the third person, something extraordinary began to happen: The room became a "we-space"—a shared field of honesty, safety, and coherence.

People began responding to each other directly. Misunderstandings dissolved. Blame softened. Two members apologized. Another admitted she had made assumptions that weren't true.

Finally, Maya said:

"We've been operating with expectations. Let's shift to agreements."

Together, they crafted a simple set of explicit agreements—not about tasks, but about how they would relate:

- Speak the unsaid before it turns into distance
- Ask to understand, not to confirm assumptions
- Tell the truth without blame or defensiveness
- Pause and reset when tension begins to rise
- Make clear agreements—and revisit them regularly

It took less than an hour. Within two weeks, everything changed. Meetings became more efficient. The launch regained momentum. The team felt lighter, more creative, more willing to take responsibility and to support one another. People smiled again. Decisions became faster. Collaboration became effortless. Maya realized something profound:

She didn't transform the team through strategy. She transformed it through relating, through presence, attunement, and creating a field where everyone could be human again.

The project eventually launched successfully, but more importantly, something deeper had shifted. The team had learned to see one another. To speak truth without fear. To create agreements instead of living in unspoken expectations. To build a shared reality rather than fight from separate ones. It became the most connected, creative, and joyful team Maya had ever led.

## TAKEAWAYS

- ✦ Conscious relating is at the heart of leadership.

  Your deepest impact is shaped not by strategy or expertise, but by the quality of the connections you create.

- ✦ Connection begins with presence.

  When you slow down, regulate your nervous system, and meet another person with genuine attention, trust emerges naturally.

- ✦ Every person lives in a separate reality.

  Understanding this dissolves blame, reduces reactivity, and opens the door to compassion, perspective-shifting, and deeper collaboration.

- ✦ Attunement transforms relationships.

  When you sense not just words but emotional tone, energy, and unspoken signals, connection becomes a living field rather than an exchange of information.

- ✦ Authenticity is more powerful than perfection.

  Speaking truth without force and listening without defense creates coherence—the foundation of psychological safety.

- ✦ Agreements replace expectations.

  Expectations create resentment; agreements create clarity, alignment, and shared responsibility.

- ✦ Creative collaboration arises from essence, not ego.

  When people feel seen, safe, and valued, their intelligence becomes collective rather than competitive.

- ✦ The heart is a leadership instrument.

  Heart-centered presence creates warmth, belonging, and a felt sense of unity that no technique can replicate.

- Human connection is the one thing AI cannot replace.

  As technology accelerates, relational intelligence becomes the defining capability of conscious leaders.

- Conscious relating is a daily practice.

  Each interaction is an opportunity to return to presence, choose openness, and co-create a field where others can thrive.

## PRACTICES

Conscious relating is not achieved through insight alone—it is cultivated through the way we show up, moment after moment. These practices are simple, repeatable, and designed to shift you from habitual, ego-driven interaction into relational presence. They are doorways into a new way of being with others.

### 1. The Pause That Creates Space

Before entering a conversation—especially one involving emotion, conflict, or complexity—pause and feel your body.

Let your breath deepen, and your attention settle into the center of your chest or belly.

This brief reset shifts you from reactivity into presence.

When you enter the space regulated, you create a field where others can settle too.

### 2. Seeing the Human Behind the Role

Choose one interaction each day, either with a colleague, partner, stranger, or team member, and intentionally notice the person behind their function.

See their humanness, not their role.

Let this recognition soften your tone, open your curiosity, and shift the relational field.

### 3. Relational Mindfulness in Conversation

During your next meaningful conversation, let part of your awareness rest on the space between you.

Sense the subtle shifts: openness, tension, alignment, hesitation.

This practice trains attunement—the ability to read the emotional and energetic landscape without jumping to conclusions or fixing anything.

Stay present to the field and let your responses arise from it rather than from habitual scripts.

### 4. Listening for Reality, Not for Response

When someone speaks, listen as if you are learning a new world.

Do not prepare your reply.

Do not correct or evaluate.

Listen to understand the reality they live in, which is different from yours.

This kind of listening dissolves defensiveness and opens relational clarity.

### 5. Speak from Center, Not from Emotion

Before you offer feedback, express a concern, or share truth, take a moment to find your center.

Feel your feet, your breath, your heart.

From this grounded orientation, speak honestly but without force.

Truth delivered from center is easier for others to receive.

Truth delivered from charge creates resistance.

### 6. Shift from Expectation to Agreement

Choose one relationship—professional or personal—where expectations are unclear or unspoken.

Initiate a brief conversation to transform those expectations into explicit agreements.

This practice strengthens trust and reduces emotional residue in relationships.

### 7. Cultivate Heart Coherence

Bring awareness to your heart area and breathe gently as if through the chest.

Think of someone you appreciate or a moment that evokes warmth.

Allow the feeling to expand.

Heart coherence stabilizes the relational field and awakens compassion—two qualities that elevate every interaction.

### 8. Practice Perspective-Shifting

In moments of disagreement, pause and ask internally:

*What might be true in their world that I cannot see yet?*

Then add a second gentle inquiry inspired by the "change of heart" principle:

*What shifts in me if I approach this with goodwill?*

These two questions open the heart, widen perspective, and make genuine understanding possible.

### 9. Create Micro-Moments of Connection

In your next interaction, intentionally create a small moment of connection. Offer a sincere greeting. Make eye contact that acknowledges presence. Express one genuine appreciation.

These micro-gestures may seem simple, but they accumulate into trust, belonging, and emotional safety. They are the soil in which collaboration and creativity grow.

### 10. Close the Day with Relational Reflection

At the end of the day, reflect on one interaction that felt aligned and one that felt contracted.

Notice what was happening in your body, breath, attention, and intention in each moment.

Without judgment, let this awareness refine how you show up tomorrow.

# CHAPTER 7
# Conscious Loving

*Power without love is reckless and abusive, and*
*love without power is sentimental and anemic.*
—Martin Luther King Jr.

In the context of conscious leadership, power refers to inner strength—the grounded capacity to uphold truth, set boundaries, act with integrity, and protect what matters. Conscious loving is the art of integrating these two forces—love and strength—into a form of leadership that elevates, stabilizes, and transforms.

It is love expressed as presence, as awareness, and as strength infused with compassion and clarity.

To love consciously is to embrace another's humanity without reservation and without judgment, and to see the beauty at their core. It is the refusal to withhold dignity, presence, or care in the face of imperfection.

In this chapter, love is not romantic affection. It is not rescuing, pleasing, avoiding conflict, or being endlessly agreeable.

I believe that at the heart of conscious leadership lies a simple but profound mission: the conscious creation of beauty, strength, and love in ourselves, in others, and out in the world. Conscious loving is the lived expression of that mission.

## What Conscious Loving Is (and What It Is Not)

Conscious loving is one of the most misunderstood—and most avoided—dimensions of leadership. In many organizational cultures, the word *love* feels out of place, even inappropriate. We are comfortable discussing strategy, performance, accountability, resilience, and execution. But love, we assume, belongs to personal life, not professional life.

And yet, if leadership is fundamentally relational, then love—understood as presence, care, truth, integrity, and genuine regard for human beings—is not only appropriate, it is indispensable.

Still, conscious loving is often confused with what it is not. It is not emotional caretaking. It is not rescuing people from discomfort, solving their problems for them, or shielding them from the very tension that growth requires. It is not sentimentality, softness without clarity, kindness without truth, or harmony purchased at the cost of integrity.

*So, what is conscious loving?*

Conscious loving is the integration of truth and care. It is the willingness to speak honestly while remaining open-hearted; to hold compassion while upholding clarity; to support growth without slipping into control or caretaking.

It is leadership that elevates rather than pleases, strengthens rather than rescues, and liberates rather than directs.

Conscious loving invites the highest in others while honoring their humanity as they grow. It recognizes the dignity, complexity, and potential in each person—even in conflict, frustration, or disappointment.

At its core, conscious loving is the art of relating from essence rather than ego. It is meeting people with presence instead of protection, and with humanity instead of judgment.

This kind of love expands people. It strengthens leadership without drifting into force and deepens relationships without collapsing into sentimentality. Conscious loving is not about being less powerful; it is about expressing power in a way that is deeply human, deeply trusted, and deeply transformative.

## The Five Expressions of Conscious Loving

Love becomes leadership through expression.

The capacities explored in earlier chapters—presence, awareness, listening, and relating—form the inner architecture of leadership. Conscious loving is what happens when those capacities come alive in relationship. These are not new skills; they are the ways love moves through a leader when presence, awareness, and compassion become embodied.

In practice, conscious loving expresses itself through five distinct yet interconnected dimensions.

### 1. Loving Presence: Being With, Not Over or Against

Loving presence is the ability to meet another person fully, without distraction, judgment, or agenda. It is the experience of being *with* someone and being attuned to their humanity rather than their role.

In loving presence, the leader's attention becomes spacious and stabilizing. People feel met rather than managed. This quality of presence creates the relational ground from which trust and connection naturally emerge.

### 2. Loving Awareness: Understanding Another's Inner World Without Losing Your Own

This expression of love integrates perspective, compassion, and boundaries. It is the capacity to sense the emotional reality of another person—their fears, hopes, interpretations, and wounds—while staying grounded in your own center.

Loving awareness honors separate realities. It asks: *What might be true in their world that I cannot yet see?*

It dissolves blame, softens reactivity, and replaces assumptions with curiosity. It creates the relational safety where truth can be spoken, and transformation can occur.

### 3. Loving Communication: Truth Delivered With Care, and Care Delivered With Clarity

Loving communication turns truth-telling into an act of integrity. It is truth that does not wound, care that remains grounded, clarity that does not dominate, and compassion that does not retreat in the face of discomfort.

This expression of love protects the dignity of the relationship while allowing difficult truths to be spoken. It strengthens the connection precisely because it refuses to trade honesty for harmony.

### 4. Loving Boundaries: Protecting What Is Sacred, Healthy, and True

In conscious leadership, boundaries are not barriers; they are expressions of love.

A boundary says: *This is what I stand for. This is what I will not compromise. This is the clarity that protects our relationship.*

Loving boundaries prevent resentment, confusion, and emotional leakage. They allow a leader to be warm without becoming permissive, clear without becoming rigid, and available without losing themselves. Boundaries are love in structural form.

### 5. Loving Devotion: Supporting the Growth, Healing, and Potential of Others

This expression of love is not caretaking or rescuing; it is calling forth.

Loving devotion is the deep commitment to another's evolution. It is believing in their potential even when they doubt it, and standing with them as they step into their highest expression.

It is the willingness to hold space for growth, offer guidance without control, and maintain faith in the deeper goodness of the human being in front of you. Loving devotion is where leadership becomes service.

## Love as Transformation

Love is not only an emotion; it is a transformative force. When expressed consciously in leadership, love reshapes the conditions in which people relate and perform—making new levels of trust, truth, and possibility available.

Love transforms because it changes the *context* of interaction. When a leader brings warmth, clarity, presence, and goodwill into a relationship, something begins to reorganize. Defensiveness softens. The nervous system settles. Curiosity awakens. People become more available to learning, honesty, and growth.

One of the first ways this transformation occurs is through psychological safety. When people feel held by a leader's grounded presence and benevolent intention, they are more willing to speak honestly, take risks, admit mistakes, and explore new ideas. This safety is not permissiveness; it is the absence of fear-driven self-protection.

Love also dissolves shame and contraction. Where judgment tightens the self, love loosens it. When someone feels seen without condemnation, the parts of them that once hid begin to relax.

Energy that was bound in self-protection becomes available for contribution and growth.

In a different way, conscious loving enables accountability. Because love is not indulgence but compassionate truth-telling, a loving leader holds high standards without resorting to humiliation or force. Accountability becomes an act of respect—an invitation to rise—rather than a mechanism of control.

Over time, love interrupts reactive patterns and awakens potential. When one person meets tension with openness instead of defensiveness, habitual dynamics lose their grip. The relational field shifts. A leader's steady faith in another's capacity becomes an internal permission for that person to grow beyond their previous limits.

Love transforms not by demanding change, but by creating the conditions in which change becomes natural. It does not overpower; it invites. It does not heal through control or force; it heals through presence.

This is why conscious loving belongs at the center of leadership. It is what turns human interaction into a catalyst for growth, belonging, and collective elevation.

## Love Through the Lens of Another's World

Love becomes wiser—and more powerful—when we recognize a fundamental truth of human experience: every person lives in a separate reality.

We do not see the world as it is; we see the world as we are: shaped by history, emotional conditioning, hopes, fears, interpretations, and nervous system patterns.[5] Understanding this shifts how love moves through leadership.

When a leader forgets that others inhabit different inner worlds, disagreement is easily personalized, and difference is experienced as a threat. Judgments form quickly. Reactivity takes hold. But when a leader remembers separate realities, love becomes more spacious. Curiosity replaces assumption. Tension becomes information rather than danger.

Loving through this lens releases the demand for sameness. Love no longer requires others to think, feel, decide, or cope as we do. When the need for sameness falls away, the impulse to correct or control softens. We begin to meet people where they actually are.

Recognizing another's inner world does not mean agreement or losing one's center. It means acknowledging the dignity of their experience without abandoning one's own grounding. Love remains clear and anchored while allowing difference to exist without threat.

Much relational harm arises from assuming intent or mistaking interpretation for truth. When leaders hold the reality of separate worlds, they carry their conclusions more lightly. Judgment loosens its grip, and understanding becomes possible.

From this awareness, perspective-shifting naturally emerges. Instead of asking, “Why are they like this?” a leader begins asking, “What might be true in their world that makes this make sense?” This ability to step outside one’s own frame without losing oneself is one of the quiet strengths of conscious leadership.

When love is grounded in the truth of separate realities, it becomes clearer because it no longer fights what it does not understand. It becomes kinder because it sees more deeply. It becomes stronger because it is not destabilized by differences. And it becomes more transformative because it meets people where they actually are.

Separate realities do not divide us; they give us the map to find one another. When leaders love through this lens, conflict becomes less personal, collaboration becomes more honest, and relationships become sacred ground for mutual evolution.

## Love and Healing in Leadership

Conscious loving is not only relational—it is healing.

Every human being carries old patterns: fears, defenses, wounds, interpretations, and emotional imprints formed long before the present moment. These patterns shape how people show up at work: how they respond to feedback, handle pressure, trust others, and protect themselves from vulnerability.

A leader who relates with conscious love becomes a regulating presence—someone whose steadiness softens reactivity, whose openness invites honesty, and whose groundedness helps others feel safe enough to grow.[7]

This is not therapy. It is not caretaking. It is not a leader becoming a savior. It is something simpler and more powerful: when a leader is attuned, present, and grounded in goodwill, the relational field changes. What was tense becomes workable. What was guarded becomes available. Truth can surface, and possibility re-enters the room.

In this sense, love becomes a form of healing—not because the leader fixes anyone, but because their presence creates the conditions in which growth becomes possible.

Love heals through attuned listening, when a person feels fully heard without being judged or rushed. Compassion allows mistakes to become learning rather than shame. Honest, caring truth invites people out of old patterns and into fuller versions of themselves. Boundaries protect dignity and prevent cycles of resentment or confusion. And faith in another's potential often awakens capacities they could not yet see in themselves.

None of this requires a leader to take on others' emotional burdens. It simply requires a leader to be present, human, and aware.

## Love, Devotion, and Higher Purpose

Love becomes transformative when it aligns with something larger than personal preference, emotion, or immediate relationship dynamics. In conscious leadership, love is not merely a feeling; it is devotion to what matters most. It is a commitment to the dignity of people, the integrity of the work, and the deeper purpose that leadership is meant to serve. Love, in this sense, is expressed through purpose.

Across wisdom traditions, love and purpose have always been inseparable. Zoroastrian teachings emphasize Good Thoughts,

Good Words, and Good Deeds as expressions of inner clarity and devotion. This is love enacted through responsibility. Sufi mystics describe love as a refining fire that purifies the heart and dissolves separation, aligning the individual with a deeper truth. Yogic and Buddhist traditions speak of compassion (*karuna*) not as sentiment, but as an active force—love that alleviates suffering, awakens wisdom, and anchors action in service.

In leadership, this dimension of love is not abstract or spiritualized. It is profoundly practical. Devotional love reveals itself through the choices a leader makes: to honor dignity under pressure, to speak truth even when it is costly, to act with integrity when no one is watching, and to serve the work in ways that uplift rather than use others.

When love is connected to higher purpose, it stabilizes a leader from within. Challenges feel less personal. Conflict becomes easier to navigate without reactivity. Decisions are guided by values rather than fear or ego. Devotion brings an inner steadiness, a quiet knowing that leadership is not only about *what* we create, but *how* we create it.

This form of love is not blind obedience to a cause. It is alignment with one's deeper truth. It is the recognition that the work we do shapes who we become, and that the way we lead shapes the inner lives of others. Devotion, in this sense, is love expressed through responsibility, integrity, and purpose.

Leaders who embody devotional love do not rely on charisma to inspire. They inspire through congruence—when who they are, how they relate, and what they stand for are visibly aligned. People trust them not because they are flawless, but because their values and actions are aligned. Their leadership serves something larger, and others can feel it.

Devotional love is the quiet strength behind conscious leadership. It is love extended beyond preference into principle, beyond relationship into purpose. It transforms leadership from a role into a calling.

## Love in the Age of AI

If conscious loving were easy, our world and our organizations would look very different. Many forces in modern life work against our capacity to love—not sentimental love, but the grounded, courageous, truth-anchored love that conscious leadership requires.

One of the greatest barriers is busyness. When leaders are rushed, overloaded, or constantly reactive, presence disappears. Without presence, love has nowhere to land. Busyness pulls us out of the heart and into efficiency, survival, and control.

Another barrier is the protective ego—the part of us that fears judgment, diminishment, or exposure. Instead of leading from essence, we lead from image. When self-protection takes precedence, connection erodes and love contracts.

Layered onto this is a hyper-digital world that increasingly mediates human contact. Communication becomes screen-based, transactional, and disembodied. We message instead of meeting, react instead of reflect, coordinate instead of relate. Many people are more connected than ever, and yet more isolated.

We now stand at the threshold of a deeper shift: the rise of artificial intelligence.

AI can process information, recognize patterns, and simulate conversation with remarkable sophistication. But it cannot love. It cannot care. It cannot attune to another human nervous system or create the felt sense of safety, dignity, and belonging that allows people to grow. These capacities remain irreducibly human.

This is why conscious loving becomes even more essential. As AI grows more capable, leaders are called to grow more human.

AI may automate work, but it cannot cultivate trust.

AI may optimize systems, but it cannot repair a fractured relationship.

AI may simulate empathy, but it cannot embody compassion.

In an AI-augmented world, leadership will be distinguished less by access to and processing of information, and more by the quality of presence leaders bring. Their warmth. Their clarity. Their willingness to meet others with care and truth. Their capacity to create belonging where fragmentation has become the norm.

Conscious loving is how leadership remains human as technology accelerates. It is how leaders ensure that as our tools evolve, our hearts must evolve with them, anchored in presence, integrity, and genuine regard for the people they serve.

Jonathan, a brilliant but impatient CEO, arrived at a coaching session visibly agitated.

"I'm done with her," he said, referring to his head of product. "She's emotional, defensive, and takes everything personally. I can't lead someone who collapses every time I give feedback."

Beneath the frustration, something quieter was present—disappointment, confusion, and a sense of rupture he hadn't fully named.

I asked him a simple question.

"What do you actually want for her?"

He paused. His jaw softened. His shoulders dropped slightly.

"I want her to succeed," he said. "She's talented. I just can't get through to her."

"Good," I said. "Now tell me—what part of *you* shows up when you speak to her?"

He looked down.

"The part that's tired," he admitted. "And frustrated. And...... the part that wants control."

In that moment, the conversation shifted from blame to awareness. Instead of replaying the conflict, we explored his internal stance: the impatience in his voice, the tightening in his chest, the speed of his reactions. We traced the subtle ways ego had taken the wheel—impatience, judgment, the belief that pressure would produce results.

Once he could see this clearly, I offered him an invitation.

"What would it look like to meet her with love—not sentiment or softness, but conscious loving: grounded presence, uncompromising honesty, and the steadiness to remain open without withdrawing or attacking?"

He leaned back.

"That's very different from what I've been doing."

We practiced. He slowed his breath. He softened his tone. He imagined standing in his center without force, speaking truth without judgment, honoring her humanity without absorbing her emotions.

He left the session with a different stance—not a tactic, but a shift in presence.

Two days later, he walked into her office. This time, he didn't lead with impatience or armor himself in authority. He simply said:

"I realize I haven't been meeting you the way you deserve. I've been impatient, and that's made it harder for you to show up fully. I want us to work together in a way that helps you succeed. Can we start again?"

She was quiet for a moment. Her eyes softened. Her shoulders relaxed.

"Thank you," she said. "I've been scared of disappointing you. That fear makes me shut down. I don't want that. I want to contribute."

The conversation that followed was one they had both been avoiding. They spoke honestly, clarified expectations, and created agreements that reduced misinterpretation and resentment.

Nothing dramatic happened. No sudden breakthrough. Just two human beings meeting one another from essence rather than ego.

Over the following weeks, the quality of their collaboration changed. She brought forward ideas she had previously withheld. He practiced patience and curiosity. Both stepped forward with greater ownership and accountability. Disagreements were met with truth and care rather than tension and reactivity.

When Jonathan returned to the coaching session, he said:

"I didn't realize how much power there is in meeting someone with love—the kind that has a spine. It changed everything, including me."

This is conscious loving: not rescuing, not pleasing, not avoiding conflict, but the willingness to meet another human being with truth, presence, and compassion so they can rise into their own strength.

## TAKEAWAYS

- Love is not softness; it is strength expressed with humanity.

  Conscious loving integrates truth, care, clarity, and warmth. It elevates others without rescuing them and supports growth without collapsing into pleasing or avoidance.

- Conscious loving is the art of relating from essence rather than ego.

  It replaces defensiveness with openness, judgment with curiosity, and performance with presence. When leaders relate from essence, others feel safe, valued, and able to bring forward their best.

- People grow in the presence of love joined with truth.

  Warmth without honesty breeds confusion; honesty without warmth breeds fear. Conscious loving holds both compassion and courage—creating relationships that become catalysts for change.

- Separate realities make love wiser.

  When leaders recognize that each person sees the world through their own inner landscape, blame softens, reactivity dissolves, and understanding becomes possible. Love honors another's worldview without losing one's center.

- A loving presence is inherently healing, but not because it fixes.

  Leaders do not heal others; they create the conditions for healing to arise. Safety, dignity, and attuned presence reorganize the nervous system and open the space for growth and integration.

- Love as a leadership force.

  Love builds trust, deepens belonging, expands creativity, and stabilizes relational systems. It turns teams into communities and collaboration into a source of energy rather than strain.

- Love as a strategic differentiator.

  In a world becoming increasingly digital and mediated by AI, love becomes a strategic differentiator.

  AI may simulate empathy or predict behavior, but it cannot love. The leaders of the future will distinguish themselves through the quality of their presence, their compassion, and their ability to open hearts and elevate human potential.

## PRACTICES

Conscious loving is expressed through practice. These micro-practices help you embody love as presence, truth, courage, and care in daily leadership.

### 1. Return to the Heart

Place attention on the center of your chest.

Soften the breath. Allow the chest to loosen and the shoulders to drop.

Feel the difference between a guarded heart and an open one—even a slight opening changes the relational field.

Let the intention arise quietly: *May I meet this moment with warmth and clarity.*

### 2. The Loving Pause

Before responding, especially in moments of tension, pause.

Feel your feet, soften the jaw, inhale slowly.

This moment of presence interrupts reactive patterns and creates space for a more loving choice.

Ask inwardly: *Am I about to react from fear, or respond from essence?*

### 3. Meeting Yourself with Warmth

Turn the same compassion you offer others toward yourself.

Acknowledge your own fears, fatigue, or frustration with kindness rather than self-judgment.

When leaders relate to themselves with love, they naturally relate to others with more generosity and steadiness. Self-regard is the foundation of loving others.

### 4. Attuning Without Absorbing

When listening to someone, feel their world, but stay anchored in your own center.

Notice their tone, pace, emotion, and underlying need.

Let your heart be open, but keep your spine steady.

Attunement is love that feels *with* another without collapsing *into* them.

### 5. Truth Through Kindness, Kindness Through Truth

When something difficult needs to be said, begin from care.

Feel the truth in your body.

Speak it with clarity and warmth at the same time.

Truth without love wounds.

Love without truth weakens.

Together, they become a force for growth.

### 6. Courageous Clarification

When expectations are vague, or assumptions begin to accumulate, pause and clarify.

Try asking:

*What do we each truly need to move forward with clarity?*

or

*What agreements would support both of us here?*

Clear agreements are acts of love that prevent resentment and promote connection.

### 7. Perspective Shifting with a Change of Heart

When feeling misunderstood, annoyed, or defensive, take a breath and ask:

*What might be true in their world that I cannot see yet?*

This simple shift—a "change of heart," as George Pransky describes—softens the mind and opens perspective.

It transforms judgment into curiosity and restores goodwill between people.

A small inner shift often dissolves large outer misunderstandings.

### 8. Extending Love into the Field

Bring someone to mind, whether it is a colleague, team member, or relationship in tension.

Hold them in your awareness with openness.

Offer a simple intention:

*May this person feel supported. May they act from their best self.*

This is not about changing them. It is about changing the *field* between you, so as to make it more spacious, humane, and receptive to truth and possibility.

CHAPTER 8

# Conscious Coaching

*If he is indeed wise, he does not bid you enter the house of his wisdom, but rather leads you to the threshold of your own mind.*
—Khalil Gibran

Most people think coaching is about helping others improve. In conscious leadership, coaching is something far deeper: It is the art of awakening another human being's wisdom, responsibility, and inner power without creating dependency or diminishing their agency.

Coaching is not directing. It is not correcting. It is not giving advice disguised as questions. It is not shaping people into who we want them to be.

Conscious coaching is a partnership of presence; a relational field where truth, curiosity, and compassion invite someone to become more fully themselves.

The coach-leader does not impose improvement; they evoke awareness. They do not push people toward outcomes; they illuminate choices. They do not rescue; they reveal. They do not carry others; they call them forward.

At its essence, conscious coaching is leadership expressed through love, strength, and beauty: love that honors the whole person with compassion, strength that challenges the ego's limiting story without diminishing the person, and beauty that inspires the emergence of their highest expression.

Coaching rests on a profound respect for human dignity:

Every person is capable, every person is creative, and every person holds their own answers—even if obscured by fear, habit, or self-doubt. The role of a conscious coach is not to provide those answers, but to help the other discover the deeper truth already waiting within them.

In this way, coaching becomes a spiritual discipline that asks for presence instead of performance, attunement instead of agenda, courage instead of comfort, and partnership instead of hierarchy. And it is profoundly generative.

When a leader coaches consciously, they do far more than solve a problem—they awaken agency, ownership, and a higher level of consciousness in the people they serve. This is why coaching is not a technique. It is a way of being.

A leader who coaches consciously becomes a catalyst for transformation, though not through force, but through presence; not through pressure, but through truth held with compassion and courage.

Conscious coaching is how leaders grow other leaders. It is how potential becomes capability, how insight becomes action, and how human beings rise into their own strength.

## What Conscious Coaching Is (and What It Is Not)

Most leaders believe they are coaching when they are actually correcting, advising, or rescuing. These patterns often arise from good intentions, but they are rooted in ego, in the impulse to fix, to solve, to direct, or to be the one who knows.

Conscious coaching begins when a leader understands the difference between guiding from ego and guiding from essence.

- Ego tries to improve people; essence awakens them.
- Ego supplies answers; essence evokes insight.
- Ego pushes for outcomes; essence illuminates choice.

But conscious coaching is not only compassionate—it is courageous.

It requires the strength to challenge assumptions people mistake for facts, to name patterns they would rather avoid, and to gently disrupt comfort zones where growth has stalled. This is not force. It is compassionate disruption; it is strength applied in service of someone's expansion, not the coach's authority.

Conscious coaching is not:

- Fixing, because fixing assumes the other person is broken
- Rescuing, because rescuing removes responsibility and creates dependence
- Advising disguised as curiosity, because it limits discovery to the coach's worldview
- Shaping people into who we want them to be,

because that serves the leader's identity rather than the person's evolution

- Leading through control or hidden expectation, because it replaces awareness with compliance

*So, what is conscious coaching?*

Conscious coaching evokes awareness, strengthens agency, and awakens inner freedom. It supports people in discovering the truth already present within them by inviting choice rather than compliance, clarity rather than confusion, and ownership rather than dependence.

It requires the leader to remain rooted in presence rather than performance, inquiry rather than assumption, and attunement rather than agenda. This stance honors human dignity by trusting that insight, capability, and choice already exist, even when temporarily obscured by fear, habit, or self-doubt.

A conscious coach becomes a catalyst, not a director; a companion in someone's expansion rather than the architect of their path. From this stance, coaching moves beyond technique and becomes a way of being.

## The Five Foundations of Conscious Coaching

Conscious coaching becomes possible when five inner capacities come together. These are not techniques to apply; they are ways of being to practice. They form the ground from which every transformative coaching conversation grows.

Each foundation reflects a core dimension of conscious leadership—presence, awareness, inquiry, strength, and empowerment—expressed in relational form.

## 1. Coaching Presence

Presence is the foundation of conscious coaching.

It is the capacity to hold a grounded, spacious field in which another person feels safe to think, feel, and reveal themselves without fear of judgment, interruption, or pressure.

This presence is not passive—it is attuned. It communicates: *I am here. I am steady. Nothing you bring will overwhelm me or make me withdraw.*

When a leader offers this quality of presence, the nervous system relaxes. Defensiveness softens. People begin to hear themselves more clearly. Insight becomes available not because it is forced, but because the conditions for clarity are finally present.

Transformation begins here—quietly, naturally, and without coercion.

## 2. Coaching Awareness

Coaching awareness is the ability to see a person beyond their behavior, beyond their fear, and beyond the story they are currently telling about themselves.

It is the capacity to perceive both the patterns that limit and the potential that wants to emerge without projecting agenda, expectation, or identity onto them.

This awareness is rooted in curiosity rather than interpretation. It asks:

- ✦ *What is trying to reveal itself here?*
- ✦ *What is trying to emerge in this person?*

Coaching awareness holds two truths at once: the small story the ego is protecting, and the larger possibility the person is being called toward. When someone feels accurately and compassionately seen without distortion or judgment, something inside them relaxes and opens. Growth becomes possible.

### 3. Coaching Inquiry

Inquiry is the art of helping someone discover what is true for them.

Not through questions that narrow the field of discovery.

Not through advice disguised as curiosity.

Not through clever prompts that quietly serve the coach's agenda.

Conscious inquiry is an expression of both love and strength. Love, because it trusts the person's inner wisdom. Strength, because it refuses to reinforce the limiting narratives that keep them small.

A powerful coaching question opens rather than narrows. It restores agency rather than creating dependence. It brings someone closer to themselves, not closer to the coach's opinion.

Inquiry is not about extracting answers. It is about illuminating awareness and insight—the kind that shifts identity, expands perspective, and awakens responsibility. At the right moment, a single honest question can change the trajectory of a life.

### 4. Coaching Challenge

Challenge is where the strength dimension of conscious leadership becomes active.

It is not confrontation, pressure, or criticism. It is the willingness to gently disrupt the ego's familiar story so a person can step into a larger version of themselves.

Coaching challenge asks:

- *Is this really who you are?*
- *What truth are you avoiding?*
- *What becomes possible if you stop protecting this narrative?*

This is not force; it is compassionate disruption. It questions assumptions people treat as facts. It names patterns they would rather not see. It creates openings where growth has been stalled by comfort or fear.

When delivered with presence and love, challenge becomes a profound act of respect—a way of saying: *I believe you are capable of more than this moment suggests.*

### 5. Coaching Awakening

The purpose of coaching is not insight alone—it is awakening.

Awakening, in this context, is the restoration of agency. It is the moment when someone remembers their own capacity, reclaims responsibility, and steps into conscious choice. It does not grant power; it reveals it. It does not create authority; it restores authorship.

A conscious coach does not empower from above. They create the conditions in which awareness deepens, responsibility strengthens, and agency re-emerges. The person begins to see that they are not merely shaped by circumstances but that they are capable of shaping what comes next.

They help others:

- See new possibilities
- Choose clarity rather than fear

- Act from ownership rather than obligation
- Trust inner wisdom more than external approval

This is where coaching becomes generative. Insight turns into action. Responsibility matures into leadership. Potential becomes lived expression.

## Coaching from Essence, Not Ego

Every coaching conversation is shaped not only by the client's mindset, but by the coach's internal state.

In each moment, the coach stands in one of two orientations: **ego or essence**.

Ego enters the conversation needing to fix, direct, prove, or be right. There is an urgency to move things forward, to resolve discomfort, or to demonstrate competence. Even when well-intentioned, ego-based coaching subtly narrows the field. It leads, corrects, or steers the conversation toward the coach's worldview.

Essence enters differently. It opens space for curiosity, inquiry, and trust in the other person's innate intelligence. Essence does not try to shape someone. It creates the conditions for self-discovery. This distinction is decisive.

Ego reacts to the story. Essence senses the deeper pattern beneath it.

Ego tries to improve people. Essence helps them remember who they are.

Coaching from essence looks and feels different. It means listening without preparing a solution. Asking without an agenda. Challenging without judgment. Reflecting without interpretation. Holding silence without anxiety. Trusting the person more than the problem.

These capacities are practical and transformative. They shift the quality of the coaching moment. When a coach stands in essence, their presence becomes regulating—steadying the nervous system, widening perspective, and helping the other reconnect with their own inner authority.

Transformation arises here not through pressure, but through the clarity that reconnects people with their own inner authority.

When leaders coach from this place, conversations become deeper, cleaner, and more liberating, not because the leader is impressive, but because they are aligned: aligned with presence rather than reactivity, with truth rather than comfort, with potential rather than performance.

Essence-based coaching reveals something fundamental: the purpose of coaching is not to provide answers, but to return people to the part of themselves that already knows.

## The Coaching Stance: Holding the Field

Coaching is not primarily a skill set. It is a stance.

Before a question is asked or an insight offered, the coach's presence is already shaping the space. People respond less to technique than to the nervous system, attention, and intention of the person in front of them. In this way, coaching is somatic and relational long before it becomes cognitive.[10]

A conscious coach does more than listen. They hold a field, a relational atmosphere in which another person can think more clearly, feel more safely, and access parts of themselves that are normally unavailable.

This stance is expressed through grounded presence, non-judgmental awareness, embodied stillness, attunement without merging, compassionate truthfulness, and spacious intention.

Grounded presence communicates stability and spaciousness—a quiet sense that nothing needs to be fixed in this moment. When the coach is steady, the client's nervous system settles.[11] Defensiveness softens. Insight becomes available.

Non-judgmental awareness creates psychological safety. It is not cold neutrality, but warm receptivity. It is seeing clearly without labeling, diagnosing, or reacting. In such an atmosphere, people no longer perform; they begin to meet themselves honestly.

Embodied stillness allows the coach to remain open in the presence of intensity. Emotional charge, confusion, or uncertainty do not provoke agitation or withdrawal. This steadiness becomes regulating. It invites the other person's system to settle as well.

Attunement without merging enables depth without entanglement. The coach senses shifts in breath, tone, and energy while remaining anchored in their own center. Understanding does not become rescuing. Empathy does not dissolve clarity.

Compassionate truthfulness integrates love and strength. Care meets the person where they are; courage names what constrains them; clarity illuminates what is possible. Transformation requires both warmth and honesty.

A spacious intention—free of agenda—keeps ownership where it belongs. The coach does not enter the conversation to prove, fix, or drive an outcome. The intention is steady and clean: to support the other in reconnecting with their own clarity and agency.

When these qualities converge, the coaching stance becomes an invisible but potent atmosphere in which inner intelligence awakens. People think more clearly when met by steadiness. They speak more honestly in the presence of non-judgment. They access courage when held with compassion. They become more creative when deeply attuned.

A conscious coach becomes a mirror, a catalyst, and a sanctuary—not because of what they do, but because of how they are. This is the alchemy that makes coaching transformational rather than transactional.

## The Power of Inquiry

Inquiry is the engine of transformation. The right question disrupts the ego, awakens awareness, and returns a person to their own wisdom. In conscious coaching, questions are not tools for extracting information; they are invitations that expand the space of possibility.

Most leaders ask questions with an agenda. They are designed to confirm assumptions, steer behavior, or guide someone toward a preferred solution. These questions may sound curious, but they narrow the field. They create performance rather than reflection, compliance rather than ownership.

Conscious inquiry is different. It arises from presence, not agenda. From curiosity, not certainty. From essence, not ego.

A powerful question does not push someone toward an outcome; it brings them inward. It interrupts automatic patterns and loosens identification with limiting narratives. It clears internal fog and restores access to choice. The result is not a better answer, but a deeper relationship with their own truth, agency, and responsibility.

Inquiry in conscious coaching is less about *what* is asked than *where* the question is asked from. When the coach is grounded, spacious, and attuned, even a simple question can initiate profound insight. When the coach is rushed, reactive, or subtly controlling, even a sophisticated question lands flat.

Transformative questions share a few essential qualities. They open rather than narrow. They reveal rather than direct. They strengthen agency rather than create dependence. They bring a person closer to themselves, not closer to the coach's opinion.

Questions such as:

- *What feels most true right now, beneath the story?*
- *What are you not saying that matters?*
- *What choice would your strongest, wisest self make here?*
- *What part of you is speaking—fear, ego, or essence?*

These questions do not solve the problem. They elevate the person.

Inquiry, practiced this way, becomes an act of devotion to another's growth. It challenges without diminishing, reveals without imposing, and opens a path for someone to step into a fuller, more authentic expression of themselves.

Through inquiry, the coach does not give answers. They help others remember the deeper truth already alive within them.

## Coaching at the Edge

Much coaching happens within familiar territory: clarifying goals, improving performance, resolving surface-level challenges. This work has value, but it rarely transforms. Transformation occurs at the edge: the threshold where certainty gives way to not-knowing, where familiar identities loosen, and where something more essential begins to emerge.

The edge is not a place of force or confrontation. It is a place of heightened presence.

At the edge, there is a strong pull toward action, explanation, or quick resolution. The ego wants movement. It wants certainty restored. Conscious coaching requires the courage to resist that pull—to slow down when moving forward feels easier, to remain present when discomfort arises, and to stay with what is unfolding without prematurely fixing, advising, or rescuing.

Here, strength takes a different form. Not strength as pressure or control, but strength as steadiness and the capacity to remain grounded in uncertainty without collapsing or hardening.

At the edge, the coach's primary instrument is not technique, interpretation, or expertise. It is presence: a presence that can hold ambiguity without anxiety, intensity without reaction, and vulnerability without intrusion. From this presence, awareness deepens, truth clarifies, and genuine transformation becomes possible.

The edge appears when a client is touching something true but not yet spoken—a value quietly compromised, a fear subtly shaping decisions, or a deeper calling that no longer fits their current identity. Often, the client senses it before they can articulate it.

These moments are rarely dramatic. Conversation may remain articulate and logical, yet the body tells a different story. Breath shortens. The voice tightens. Energy contracts. Something beneath the words begins to stir.

The edge is subtle and sensitive. It exists in the narrow space between comfort and overwhelm.[12] Move too gently, and familiar patterns protect themselves. Push too forcefully, and the nervous system shifts into defense, thus narrowing perception and cutting off access to insight.

Conscious coaching is not about dragging someone out of their comfort zone, nor about protecting them from discomfort. It is about sensing the edge with precision—inviting just enough stretch to awaken awareness without tipping into panic, collapse, or self-protection.

At the edge, the urge to intervene is strong. The coach may feel pulled to reassure, reframe, interpret, or guide the client back toward familiar ground. These impulses are often well-intended but can limit growth at the very moment it is trying to emerge.

Coaching at the edge is the discipline of staying without steering. It is the capacity to remain present with what is emerging without rushing to reduce discomfort or redirect the experience. The coach holds the space steady enough for the client to stay in contact with their own truth without collapsing into comfort or escalating into pressure.

This stance is active and embodied: grounded, alert, and deeply attentive. The coach listens not only to words, but to breath, energy, pacing, and subtle shifts in presence. From this steadiness, intuitive insight becomes available—a refined perception shaped by attunement.

Inquiry at the edge is deliberate and precise. Questions are not used to move the client somewhere else, but to illuminate what is already here. Often, a single well-timed question or a moment of silence opens more than a sequence of clever interventions.

By staying without steering, the coach allows insight to arise from within the client rather than being imposed from outside. What emerges is not compliance or relief, but ownership. Not direction, but discovery.

At these threshold moments, the body often signals what the words conceal. The nervous system shifts toward protection.

Perception tightens. Without awareness, the client may retreat into explanation, justification, or subtle redirection away from what feels uncomfortable but true.

A conscious coach tracks this—not analytically, but somatically. Grounded in their own breath, they attune to the client's.

By remaining regulated, spacious, and steady, the coach stabilizes the relational field. Often, without instruction or intervention, the client's breathing softens as well. As the nervous system settles, perception widens and access to choice returns. Insight comes after regulation, not before it.[11]

Coaching at the edge also demands inner work from the coach. It requires the capacity to remain present with silence, ambiguity, and one's own discomfort, including the impulse to be helpful, insightful, or reassuring. At the edge, the temptation to intervene often arises not from the client's need, but from the coach's unease.

This is where self-trust becomes essential: trust that awareness itself is transformative, that the client's inner intelligence knows how to move forward when given space, and that presence is doing more than technique ever could.

The coach's task is not to manufacture insight, but to hold the conditions in which insight can arise naturally.

When done well, coaching at the edge feels quiet and precise as well as honest, grounded, and deeply real. In retrospect, clients often recognize these moments as turning points: quiet thresholds where something essential was finally allowed to surface.

A senior executive once came into a coaching session composed, articulate, and clear about what he wanted to discuss. On the surface, the issue was straightforward: a strategic decision he needed to make, a tradeoff between growth and stability. He spoke confidently, outlining risks, timelines, and scenarios.

As he spoke, I noticed something else happening.

His breath became shallow. His voice tightened slightly whenever he mentioned one particular option. Each time he approached it, he redirected the conversation back toward analysis and justification. The words were polished, but the body was not at ease.

As the session slowed, a long pause emerged.

I noticed the urge to fill the silence, but chose not to act on it.

There was no question to ask, no insight to offer. Just space.

After a few moments, he exhaled deeply—the first full breath he had taken in several minutes. His shoulders dropped. Then, quietly, he said, "I keep telling myself this is about strategy, but it's not. I'm afraid of what this choice will cost me."

Nothing needed to be added.

In that moment, the conversation shifted. Not because anything was explained or reframed, but because the truth had room to surface. What followed was not urgency or problem-solving, but a more honest contact with what mattered most to him.

Weeks later, he reflected that the most important part of the session was not the decision he made, but the way he learned to recognize when he was avoiding himself and how to pause long enough to listen.

## From Edge to Integration

Touching the edge is where the real coaching begins.

When a client encounters a deeper truth—a realization, a shift in perspective, a quiet inner knowing—there is often a reflex to move quickly into action. The coach may feel compelled to ask, *So what will you do?* or *How will this change your behavior?* But urgency at this stage can collapse insight back into performance.

Conscious coaching honors integration. Integration is the process by which insight settles into the nervous system, reorganizes identity, and gradually reshapes choice. It cannot be rushed without losing depth. Often, the most meaningful outcome of an edge moment is not a decision, but a new relationship to self with more honesty, more responsibility, and more inner freedom.

The coach's role here is subtle and precise. Rather than extracting commitments or action items, the coach helps the client remain connected to what has shifted. This may mean naming the quality of the insight, reflecting a change in energy or presence, or simply allowing space for the experience to land.

Action, when it comes, emerges from alignment rather than pressure.

When integration is honored, choices become clearer and more grounded. Decisions arise less from fear, habit, or external expectation, and more from coherence between values, intention, and behavior. In this way, conscious coaching does more than solve problems; it strengthens agency and reshapes the way choices are made.

This is where coaching moves beyond performance and into leadership. Not leadership as role or authority, but leadership as authorship—the capacity to act from awareness rather than reaction, and from truth rather than conditioning.

## Cultivating Awareness and Self-Trust

At its core, conscious coaching cultivates awareness and self-trust.

Through conscious coaching, clients begin to recognize choice where habit once ruled, and presence where reaction once dominated. They become more attentive to their inner experience and less compelled by automatic patterns. Over time, they learn to notice what is shaping their decisions—fear, conditioning, or something deeper—and to pause long enough for a wiser response to emerge.

This is the quiet power of conscious coaching.

The coach does not become a source of answers, motivation, or direction. Instead, the coach supports the client in strengthening their relationship with their own inner wisdom and intelligence—their capacity to sense truth, regulate themselves under pressure, and act from alignment rather than compulsion.

As this capacity develops, something subtle but profound shifts. Clients stop outsourcing clarity. They listen more carefully to themselves. They recognize the difference between reacting from habit and responding from a deeper, steadier place within.

This kind of coaching does not create dependence. It cultivates self-trust.

When practiced well, conscious coaching eventually makes itself unnecessary—not because growth is complete, but because the client has learned how to listen, choose, and lead from their own inner authority.

## TAKEAWAYS

- Conscious coaching begins with presence.

  The coach's primary instrument is not technique or advice, but the steadiness and quality of attention they bring into the space.

- Transformation occurs at the edge.

  Real growth happens at the threshold between comfort and overwhelm, where awareness expands without triggering defense.

- The edge requires precision.

  Conscious coaching invites just enough stretch to surface truth while preserving safety, dignity, and regulation.

- Staying without steering is a discipline.

  Rather than fixing, rescuing, or directing, the coach holds space steadily enough for insight to emerge from within the client.

- The aim is agency and self-trust.

  By strengthening a client's capacity to listen inwardly and choose from alignment rather than habit, conscious coaching cultivates autonomy instead of dependence.

## PRACTICES

These practices train the inner discipline from which conscious coaching arises. They strengthen steadiness, perception, and self-trust in real time.

### 1. Practicing the Pause

When a conversation deepens—when something meaningful, uncertain, or unformed appears—resist the reflex to respond.

Notice the impulse to clarify, reassure, fix, or demonstrate value. Instead, remain steady. Anchor in your breath. Feel your body. Allow the silence to work.

Silence here is not withdrawal; it is precision.

After the pause, observe what shifts in the client, whether it is breath, tone, clarity, or ownership. Often, what emerges in this space is deeper than any immediate question could reach.

This practice develops discernment: knowing when to speak and when to hold.

### 2. Tracking the Edge

Shift part of your attention from content to physiology.

Watch for shortened breath, tightened tone, shifting posture, or energetic contraction. These often signal the edge where growth is near, but protection may activate.

Instead of pushing forward, adjust pace. Create space.

Ask internally:

*Is this stretch productive, or tipping into defense?*

This practice refines your ability to challenge without overwhelming.

### 3. Leading with Regulation

Enter every session regulated.

Before beginning, take several steady breaths and settle your body. During the conversation, return to that anchor whenever you feel impatience, pressure to move forward, or the impulse to intervene.

Your nervous system shapes the coaching space more than your questions do.

When you remain grounded, clarity stabilizes.

This practice builds leadership maturity: steadiness under emotional intensity.

### 4. Reflecting After the Session

After each conversation, review the field, not just the content.

*Where did you feel compelled to rescue, direct, or prove?*

*Where did you hold steady?*

*Where did insight arise naturally?*

Notice patterns without judgment.

Over time, this reflection strengthens your ability to coach from essence rather than ego.

# PART III

# Leading with Impact

## CHAPTER 9

# Conscious Choice

*Between stimulus and response, there is a space.*
*In that space is our power to choose our response.*
*In our response lies our growth and our freedom.*
—Viktor E. Frankl

It shows up as the pause before you speak, the breath before you act, the subtle hesitation between impulse and response. In that unmeasured space lies real power. Lives, organizations, and cultures are shaped less by circumstance than by the quality of choice made in those moments of awareness.

As a leader, you stand at these inner crossroads more often than you realize.

Some choices are visible: which strategy to pursue, who to hire or release, what direction to take the organization. Others are subtle and internal: whether to listen or defend, to open or control, to trust or retreat. In each moment, something within you chooses which self will lead—the self shaped by fear and habit, or the self guided by presence and purpose.

Most people experience choice as a mental act—an evaluation of options, risks, and outcomes. Conscious choice begins deeper than analysis. It begins in awareness itself.

The essential question is not only *"What should I choose?"* but *"From where in me is this choice arising?"* That question determines not just what decision is made, but who we become in the act of choosing.

When decisions arise from reactivity, they reinforce familiar patterns such as tension in the body, pressure in the mind, the impulse to protect, prove, or control. Speed often masquerades as strength, yet unexamined speed is frequently fear in motion. Conscious leaders learn to honor the space between impulse and action. In that pause, they sense, breathe, and listen—allowing intelligence to surface not only from the mind, but from the deeper knowing of the body and heart.

Every conscious choice is an act of creation. It ripples outward through conversations, teams, and systems, shaping the emotional and ethical climate around us. A single pause can transform a meeting. A decision made from alignment rather than fear can redirect a culture for years.

To choose consciously is to recognize leadership as a creative act. It is to move from habit to intention, from reaction to response, from egoic striving to essence-led action. Freedom does not come from having more options, but from having more awareness within each option.

When you slow down enough to sense the still point before each choice, you enter the domain of creation. From there, leadership is no longer about reacting to life, but about participating in shaping it.

Conscious choice is where intention and stance converge. Intention provides direction—the inner orientation of who we choose to be. Stance provides stability—the grounded presence from which we meet reality. But neither intention nor stance shapes the world until it becomes choice. Choice is the moment intention enters action and stance meets consequence. It is where philosophy becomes behavior, and awareness becomes creation.

This chapter explores the anatomy of conscious choice: what precedes it, what distorts it, and how it can be cultivated. We will examine how awareness, emotion, ego, and intention influence every decision; how to align the intelligence of head, heart, and gut; and how each conscious choice becomes a seed that shapes not only outcomes, but character.

The journey begins in the pause—the quiet threshold where your next choice awaits.

## Awareness Precedes Choice

Every conscious act begins with awareness. Before a decision can be transformed, it must first be witnessed. Awareness is the light that reveals the inner landscape, which includes our patterns, fears, desires, and assumptions. Without that light, unseen forces shape our behavior. We do not choose; we react.

Most leaders assume that choice begins when options appear. In truth, the process starts earlier, before options, before analysis, before decision. Awareness is the pre-choice. It is the inner pause in which automatic reaction loosens and genuine options become visible.

Modern neuroscience supports this understanding. Research by Richard Davidson and colleagues suggests that practices cultivating awareness strengthen the prefrontal cortex—the region associated with regulation, empathy, and long-term perspective—while reducing reactivity in the amygdala, the brain's threat center.[1] As awareness increases, emotional turbulence settles, and access to choice expands. Daniel Siegel describes this as entering the "plane of possibility"—a state in which response replaces reflex.[2]

Awareness, then, is not passive observation. It is an active intelligence. It changes what happens next. The moment something is seen clearly, it is no longer running unconsciously.

It allows leaders to notice the subtle signals that precede every choice: a tightening in the chest before saying yes, a surge of defensiveness before responding to feedback, the urge to fill silence with control. These signals are not problems to suppress; they reveal what is about to shape the decision. When noticed, they create space for choice. When ignored, they drive behavior.

Consider a leader entering a tense meeting. Without awareness, the body absorbs the room's anxiety. Breath shortens. Tone hardens. The mind searches for control. With awareness, the leader notices the tension and remains present with it. That single shift changes the quality of what follows—what is said, how listening unfolds, when action is taken. The response emerges from steadiness rather than reactivity.

Awareness precedes choice because it is the condition that makes choice possible. Without it, leadership is governed by habit and emotional momentum. With it, leaders step into authorship and are able to sense what is happening within before acting in the world. Over time, this capacity strengthens through small, consistent acts of noticing: pausing before replying to a charged message, feeling the body before entering a difficult conversation, observing inner tone before deciding.

Each moment of awareness expands freedom. When it is

absent, leadership defaults to reaction. When it is present, leadership becomes creation.

## Reaction vs. Response

Every moment offers a choice: to react from conditioning or to respond from awareness.

Reaction is automatic—fast, defensive, rooted in survival. It arises from the nervous system before conscious thought has a chance to engage. Response, by contrast, is intentional. It emerges from presence and allows clarity, creativity, and choice to enter the moment. The difference between reaction and response is the difference between being driven by fear and acting from awareness.

When something triggers us, whether it is a tense meeting, an unexpected challenge, or a difficult personality, the body reacts first. The amygdala, the brain's alarm center, activates before the thinking brain can fully process what is happening. Heart rate increases. Breath shortens. Muscles tense. The body prepares to fight, flee, or freeze.

If we act from this state, leadership becomes a mirror of reactivity. We speak sharply, withdraw prematurely, or double down on control, often in an unconscious attempt to restore a sense of safety.

Yet even in these moments, a deeper intelligence is available. By noticing the body and breathing consciously, we bring awareness back online. As the nervous system settles, access to choice returns. From this place, we can respond rather than react.

Reaction is driven by control or protection; response is guided by clarity and alignment.

Reaction defends identity; response expresses essence.

The movement from reaction to response is the first visible expression of conscious choice. It marks the shift from being driven by circumstance to participating in creation.

You may recall Jack, the CEO, introduced earlier in *Conscious Breath*—a driven, visionary leader whose intensity often spilled into frustration. In those days, he learned the power of conscious breathing to regulate his emotions. What began as a way to calm his body became something deeper: a doorway to conscious choice.

As Jack practiced awareness, he started to notice how quickly his body reacted when things didn't go as planned—a missed deadline, a disappointing report, a careless comment. His chest tightened, his tone hardened, and before realizing it, he was already in reaction mode. Each outburst left a residue of tension and aggression in the room, an invisible field of pressure that stifled openness.

One afternoon, during a critical strategy session, he caught himself mid-reaction. A presentation had gone poorly, and the familiar wave of irritation surged. But this time, he paused. He felt the tightness, took a breath, and silently asked, *What is needed here?*

That brief moment of awareness shifted everything. Instead of correcting or criticizing, he asked a question: "What do you think we're missing here?" The room softened. His team leaned in. A creative dialogue emerged where defensiveness once lived.

After the meeting, one of his managers said, "Jack, you handled that differently today. It felt. . . . . . calm." Jack smiled. He had made a different choice—not because he suppressed emotion, but because he *saw* it before it owned him.

Over time, this awareness became his leadership practice. He realized that his old reactions were rooted in fear—the fear of losing control, of not being good enough, of being let down. These fears once drove him to micromanage and overcorrect. Now, each time he noticed the urge to react, he asked himself, *Who do I want to be right now?*

That question became his compass.

Jack's leadership shifted from reaction to response, from control to creation. Meetings grew lighter, ideas flowed more freely, and trust began to rebuild. His company didn't just perform better—it felt better. The culture itself was breathing again.

What changed wasn't Jack's strategy; it was his consciousness. He had moved from being a reactor of circumstances to a creator of outcomes.

This is the essence of conscious leadership: pausing long enough to reclaim the space between stimulus and response and choosing who we become in that space.

Reaction and response reflect two deeper orientations of consciousness: victim and owner. The victim mindset says, "Things happen to me." The owner mindset says, "Things happen through me."

Reactive leaders interpret setbacks as personal assaults or external injustices. Their language reveals it: "They made me angry." "There's nothing I can do." Power is transferred outward.

Conscious leaders operate from ownership. They recognize that while circumstances cannot always be controlled, their relationship to them can be chosen. They pause, breathe, reflect, and act from clarity rather than reflex.

Reaction says, "I can't help it."

Response says, "I choose how to meet this."

Reaction says, "This is happening to me."

Response says, "This is happening through me."

Ownership is creative responsibility: the willingness to meet each moment with awareness and choice.

Jack's story is every leader's story. We all face moments when emotion surges before awareness catches up. The work is not to eliminate reaction, but to shorten its lifespan and to meet it with breath, awareness, and ownership.

The world does not need more reactive leaders. It needs responsive creators and leaders who act from presence rather than fear.

## The Ego's Hidden Hand

Even after we learn to pause, breathe, and respond, something quieter still shapes our choices.

It is the hidden architect behind much of our behavior: the ego.

Not the loud ego of arrogance, but the subtle, protective identity that whispers, *I must prove, control, or defend in order to be safe.*

The ego's intentions are not malicious; they are ancient. It evolved to protect us in a world shaped by threat and survival. But in the modern landscape of leadership, where strength is measured by awareness, coherence, and trust, these same strategies quietly limit growth.

The ego operates through compensatory acts: attempts to fill an inner sense of lack with outer achievements.

It drives the leader who overworks to feel valuable. The executive who avoids conflict to remain liked. The founder who micromanages to stay indispensable.

Each behavior can appear rational, even effective. Yet beneath it lies fear: fear of inadequacy, fear of rejection, fear of losing control.

Ego-driven choices often succeed in the short term, but fragment integrity over time. They generate results without fulfillment, success without peace. The outer world may reward them, while the inner world grows restless.

Conscious leadership begins when these patterns are no longer unconscious; when the leader can see the ego's hand at work without being ruled by it.

One of the ego's favorite disguises is control. It whispers that safety lies in certainty; that if we can predict, manage, and plan every detail, we can eliminate risk and secure success.

Planning and foresight are essential to leadership. But when the need for certainty is driven by fear of losing control or credibility, control narrows perception and constrains possibility.

Conscious leadership requires something more subtle: the capacity to remain present within uncertainty; to plan rigorously without clinging, to prepare carefully without tightening, and to lead with clarity even when outcomes cannot be guaranteed.

Control arises from fear; clarity arises from presence. The ego seeks control to protect its image; essence seeks alignment to serve what is true.

When leaders are attached to control, their choices narrow. They hire those who agree rather than those who challenge. They cling to familiar strategies rather than sensing what wants to emerge. They prioritize outcomes over alignment, approval over authenticity.

The paradox is that the more we grasp for control, the more influence we lose. True authority arises not from control, but from integrity when inner conviction and outward action move as one.

As one CEO once reflected, "When I stopped managing everything and focused instead on clarity of intention, people started taking ownership on their own."

The ego does not always appear as pride or dominance. Often, it wears softer masks:

- The Pleaser saying yes to be liked, even when it costs integrity.
- The Perfectionist striving for flawlessness to avoid criticism.
- The Rescuer fixing others to feel indispensable.
- The Rationalizer using logic to justify avoidance or denial.

Each of these roles is a reaction, a way to preserve identity. But identity is not essence. The more we defend who we think we are, the less space we have for our true selves to emerge.

When ego patterns are seen clearly, they do not need to be fought. Awareness dissolves them by exposing their source. In that moment, choice returns.

Ego-driven leadership revolves around image—how we appear. Conscious leadership arises from essence—how we are.

When choices are made to protect image, they serve reputation. When made from essence, they serve truth. The shift begins with a simple question: *Am I making this decision to prove something, or to create something?*

Proving is driven by fear and scarcity. Creating arises from alignment with essence and purpose.

A leader guided by essence does not need to defend their worth; they express it. They lead not to be admired, but to serve what is real and meaningful.

When leaders choose from awareness rather than defense, leadership stops revolving around identity and begins radiating from essence.

This is the quiet revolution of conscious choice: to act not from who you think you are, but from who you truly are.

## Intention Over Goal

Goals define what we want to accomplish; intentions define how we choose to act. A goal is something we aim to achieve. An intention is the inner orientation from which we act. One focuses on results; the other shapes the quality of who we become in pursuing them.

Modern leadership glorifies goals. We are taught to define targets, measure success, and push relentlessly toward outcomes. But when achievement is pursued without awareness, even the most impressive goals can produce success without fulfillment.

Many leaders reach their objectives and still feel disconnected. They arrive at the summit only to find the view empty. Their goals were clear, but their intentions were unconscious. Conscious leadership reverses the sequence.

Before asking *What do I want to achieve?* it asks: *Who do I choose to be as I act?*

Intention precedes authentic impact. It infuses action with meaning and transforms success from something pursued into something expressed.

A goal lives in the realm of outcome, which is measurable and external.

An intention lives in the realm of essence, which is experiential and internal.

- ✦ The goal says: *Increase revenue by 20%.*
- ✦ The intention says: *Lead with clarity, trust, and collaboration.*
- ✦ The goal says: *Run a marathon.*
- ✦ The intention says: *Cultivate discipline and joy in movement.*

Both matter. But only intention ensures that the path to the goal strengthens rather than drains the person walking it.

When goals arise from clear intentions, achievement becomes an expression of essence rather than compensation.

The ego sets goals to prove something—worth, competence, importance.

Essence forms intentions to express something—beauty, strength, love.

- ✦ Ego says: *I need to win.*
- ✦ Essence says: *I choose to contribute.*
- ✦ Ego says: *I must control the outcome.*
- ✦ Essence says: *I will choose how I show up, regardless of the outcome.*

Ego-driven goals create tension. Essence-driven intentions create integration. One fragments; the other unifies.

When leaders pursue goals without intention, success can coexist with exhaustion and disconnection. When leaders act from clear intention, even imperfect outcomes feel meaningful because they are aligned with who they are.

Sophie, the head of marketing for a global brand, had built her career on disciplined execution. Her teams respected her focus but feared her intensity. Metrics ruled every conversation.

When the company narrowly missed its annual target, Sophie responded by pushing harder. Morale dropped. Creativity stalled.

At an executive retreat, she was asked a simple question:

"What was your intention in leading this year?"

After a long pause, she answered quietly, "If I'm honest . . . I was leading to avoid failing."

That moment changed everything.

She realized her goals were driven by fear, not purpose. She gathered her team and named a new intention: *to lead with creativity and trust, not pressure.*

Meetings shifted. Energy lifted. Ideas returned.

The following year, results improved, but more importantly, the culture did.

Sophie later reflected:

"When I aligned my energy with intention, the numbers followed."

Intentions act as a compass when outcomes are uncertain.

Unlike goals, which live in the future, intentions live in the present. They can be renewed before a conversation, a meeting, or a difficult decision.

Goals define destination. Intentions define direction. Awareness ensures alignment.

Conscious leaders do not abandon goals—they infuse them with intention. They understand that leadership is not only about results, but about the quality of consciousness those results emerge from.

Every decision becomes a question of alignment:

- *Does this action express who I am and what I stand for?*
- *Does it create more beauty, strength, and love in the world?*

When intention guides choice, even setbacks become teachers. Experience is no longer something to overcome, but something to integrate.

To lead from intention is to lead from essence. It is to choose not only success, but who you become in the process.

## Choice as Creation

Every choice we make is an act of creation. It may appear ordinary—a decision in a meeting, an email reply, a hiring call—but each choice sets something in motion. Every *yes* and every *no* sends ripples outward through people, systems, and time.

The power of conscious leadership lies in recognizing this creative capacity.

When awareness, intention, and action align, choices stop being reactions to life and become expressions of creation.

Unconscious choices repeat the past. Conscious choices invent the future.

The space between stimulus and response—the pause explored earlier—is not empty. It is alive with possibility. In that space, we do not merely select between options; we generate new ones.

When a leader pauses and reconnects with intention, choice arises from presence rather than habit. From this state, decisions are no longer driven by fear or conditioning, but by alignment.

Choice is not a single moment in time. It is a field of awareness through which creation unfolds. The quality of that field determines the quality of what is created.

If the field is shaped by fear, choices generate fear. If it is shaped by trust, choices generate trust. If it is shaped by beauty, choices generate beauty. Whatever energy we choose *from* becomes the energy we create *with*.

Every leader, whether consciously or not, is shaping reality through their choices.

When a CEO chooses transparency over secrecy, trust grows. When a manager chooses curiosity over judgment, psychological safety forms. When a founder chooses stewardship over short-term gain, sustainability emerges.

In this sense, leadership is less about authority and more about authorship. Each conscious choice writes a line in the living story of the organization. Over time, those lines become culture, a reflection of the leadership team's inner state made visible.

As one executive once said, "I thought my decisions shaped the business. Now I see they shape the people who shape the business." This is what it means to lead as a creator.

The impact of a single conscious act often extends far beyond what we can see. A pause before judgment can preserve a relationship. A moment of courage can restore confidence. A choice made with integrity can ripple through teams and generations.

You may never witness the full reach of your choices, but their influence is no less real. Yet conscious creation does not end at intention.

Even well-intentioned choices can produce unforeseen consequences. A decision made with care may still create confusion. Feedback offered sincerely may still trigger defensiveness. Intention and impact are not always the same.

For this reason, conscious choice requires awareness not only in the moment of decision, but over time. It asks leaders to stay present to what their choices create—to observe, learn, and adjust.

True conscious creation is iterative. We act. We observe what unfolds. We adjust. Awareness sustains what intention begins.

Creation does not arise from force. It arises when intention is clarified, awareness is maintained, and courage is exercised in the moment of decision. Then choice becomes authorship rather than reaction.

This is not about controlling outcomes. It is about participating consciously in what unfolds, in listening for what is emerging rather than imposing what the ego demands.

You do not need certainty to make a conscious choice. You need alignment in the moment you act. From alignment, creation unfolds—not perfectly, but coherently.

This is the power of conscious choice: decisions made from presence do not merely solve problems. They shape character, culture, and consequence over time.

## Integrating Head, Heart, and Gut

A conscious choice does not arise from intellect alone. It arises from coherence, when mind, heart, and body align with essence.

Leaders often default to one center of intelligence over the others: the head for logic, the heart for empathy, or the gut for instinct. Each is valuable. None is sufficient on its own. Wisdom emerges when these three forms of knowing converge into a single, integrated awareness.

The head asks: *Is it clear?*

The heart asks: *Is it kind?*

The gut asks: *Is it true?*

When all three respond in alignment, choice feels grounded, calm, and trustworthy.

The head offers clarity and perspective. It analyzes patterns, weighs implications, and helps leaders navigate complexity. Yet when over-relied upon, it seeks control through thinking and can disconnect decision-making from lived reality.

The heart brings meaning and connection. It senses emotional truth and relational impact, expanding awareness beyond efficiency into humanity. Decisions made without the heart may be effective, but they often fail to build trust and commitment.

The gut carries instinctive intelligence and courage.[3] It registers truth somatically, often before the mind can articulate it. When ignored, leaders lose access to their deepest sense of rightness—the quiet inner "yes" or "no" that precedes explanation.

Conscious leadership requires coherence among these centers. When they align, decision-making feels fluid and whole. When they conflict, inner dissonance arises; not as a problem, but as information. That tension is a signal that alignment has not yet been reached.

Many leaders have experienced moments when the mind justified a choice the body resisted. That resistance is not weakness; it is wisdom asking for attention.

By slowing down enough to sense all three centers, leaders invite the full spectrum of intelligence into their choices. Information becomes wisdom. Wisdom becomes action.

During a leadership retreat, a senior executive faced a defining decision: whether to accept a lucrative acquisition offer that promised short-term gains but compromised the company's core values.

Logically, the deal made sense. Her head said yes. Emotionally, her heart tightened. Somatically, her gut signaled misalignment. She paused and allowed each center to speak.

The head acknowledged the numbers.

The heart recognized the cost to culture.

The gut carried the courage to say no.

When she declined the offer, she felt immediate clarity and peace. Months later, the acquiring company collapsed under internal dysfunction. Her decision had protected not only financial stability but also integrity.

She later reflected, "That choice didn't come from strategy—it came from alignment. My body and heart knew before my mind could explain it."

Integrating head, heart, and gut requires presence. It develops through attention and lived awareness.

Before a consequential choice, pause and sense:

- What do I *know*?
- What do I *feel*?
- What do I *sense*?

If alignment is absent, wait. Breathe. Listen. Coherence cannot be forced—it must be allowed.

When alignment arrives, it is unmistakable: grounded, expansive, and calm. Choice becomes less effortful. You are no longer forcing choice through analysis; a clear sense of knowing begins to guide you.

When head, heart, and gut move together, leadership becomes whole. Decisions made from that alignment generate trust, clarity, and stability in the systems they touch.

## The Ripple Effect

Every choice we make sends ripples through the field of life.

Even the smallest acts—how we listen, how we respond, how we show up—carry an imprint that shapes the world around us. Leadership is never isolated. It unfolds within a living ecosystem of cause and effect, intention and impact, consciousness and creation.

We are constantly co-authoring reality through our presence. In every organization, a leader's inner state quietly transmits to others. When a leader is anxious, the system tightens. When a leader is grounded and clear, that steadiness spreads. Emotions are profoundly social. Research on emotional contagion shows that mood and presence shape trust, creativity, and performance across teams.[4]

Who you are being shapes what you say and what you do.

Presence is the true amplifier of leadership. It operates beneath words and strategies. When you act from awareness, people feel it, even if they cannot name it. Presence steadies others in uncertainty, opens space in tense moments, and restores trust when systems strain.

A conscious choice does not end when it is made. Its effects unfold across time.

A single conversation can alter someone's sense of worth. A moment of courage can redirect a culture. History itself is shaped by such moments—small acts of alignment that ripple outward beyond their origin.

When Gandhi chose nonviolence, it was not a tactic; it was a state of being. That inner alignment resonated far beyond its moment, shaping generations. It stands as a reminder that presence, when coherent, carries extraordinary power.

And yet, conscious leadership also requires humility.

Intention and impact are not always aligned. A leader may act with care yet create confusion; offer honesty yet trigger fear. Conscious choice, therefore, asks us not only to act with awareness but to remain attentive to what our actions become over time.

This is how creation turns into stewardship. We stay present to the ripples we set in motion—listening, learning, and adjusting with responsibility and compassion. This responsibility has never been greater.

For the first time in human history, we are creating forms of intelligence that can amplify intention at an exponential scale. Artificial intelligence is not inherently benevolent or destructive—it reflects the consciousness of those who shape it.

If our choices are driven by fear, control, or scarcity, technology will magnify those qualities. If they are guided by wisdom, compassion, and service, it will magnify those instead.

AI marks not only a technological turning point, but a moral and existential reckoning. It demands that humanity evolve its consciousness as rapidly as it advances its tools.

The future will not be determined by algorithms alone, but by the awareness behind them.

To live and lead consciously is to recognize the sacred responsibility embedded in every choice. We are not merely influencing outcomes—we are shaping the collective field through the quality of our presence.

This responsibility is a privilege. When we act from ego, our ripples create distortion. When we act from essence, our ripples create harmony. Over time, those ripples weave into the larger current of human evolution. Conscious choice is not only personal, it is planetary.

And when leadership is rooted in awareness, guided by intention, and sustained by love, it leaves behind more than results. It shapes the future through every choice.

## TAKEAWAYS

- Awareness is the birthplace of choice.

  Every conscious decision begins with noticing what is arising within us before we act. Awareness creates space, and space makes freedom possible.

- Between stimulus and response lies creative power.

  In the pause between what happens and how we respond, possibility expands. The more present we are in that space, the more intentional and generative our choices become.

- Reaction is conditioning; response is freedom.

  Reaction repeats the past in the name of safety. Response arises from awareness and opens new outcomes. Conscious leaders shorten the lifespan of reactivity and reclaim authorship in the moment.

- Ownership transforms reality.

  Victim consciousness says, "This is happening to me." Ownership says, "This is happening through me." True power comes not from control, but from remaining awake and responsible within each circumstance.

- The ego seeks to prove; essence seeks to express.

  Ego-driven choices protect image. Essence-driven choices express inner alignment and integrity. When leaders act from essence, their decisions reflect truth rather than defense.

- Intention guides direction; goals define destination.

  Goals focus effort. Intention anchors the leader. When goals arise from clear intention, achievement strengthens rather than drains the person pursuing it.

- Choice is creation.

  Every decision sends ripples through people, systems, and time. The consciousness behind a choice shapes its impact as much as the action itself.

- Intention and impact must both be held.

  Conscious leaders stay attentive not only to what they intend, but to what their choices create. They observe, learn, and adjust with humility and care.

- Wisdom emerges through alignment.

  Discernment strengthens when head, heart, and gut move together; when clarity, compassion, and courage converge into grounded knowing.

- Leadership is transmission.

  Who you are being shapes what you say and what you do. Presence silently conditions trust, culture, and performance.

- Conscious creation carries profound responsibility.

  In an age of exponential technologies, especially AI, the future will reflect the consciousness of its creators.

- To choose consciously is to lead as a creator.

  Each decision shapes not only outcomes, but character and culture. Conscious leaders create beauty, strength, and love in themselves, in others, and out in the world.

## PRACTICES

These practices cultivate the inner conditions from which conscious choice becomes possible.

They are designed to strengthen awareness, allowing action to arise from alignment rather than habit.

### 1. Awareness Before Action

Before an important decision—or whenever you feel emotionally charged—pause for a single conscious breath.

Let attention drop into the body. Notice what is already here. Then ask quietly:

- *What am I feeling right now?*
- *What assumption or story is shaping this moment?*
- *Am I reacting, or responding?*

Do not try to fix anything. Simply notice. Often, awareness alone changes the trajectory of the decision.

As Viktor Frankl reminds us:

*"Between stimulus and response, there is a space. In that space is our power to choose our response. In our response lies our growth and our freedom."*

### 2. Seeing the Ego in Motion

Over the course of a week, bring gentle curiosity to moments where you feel compelled to:

- Prove yourself
- Defend your position

- Control an outcome
- Be liked or approved of

When one of these impulses appears, pause and ask:

- *What am I trying to protect or prove right now?*
- *If you weren't trying to protecting anything, what would feel most true?*

This practice replaces self-judgment with self-understanding. Each moment of recognition loosens the ego's grip and restores choice.

### 3. Three-Center Alignment

Before a significant conversation or decision, take two quiet minutes to check in with three centers of intelligence:

- **Head:** *What do I know? What facts or patterns are clear?*
- **Heart:** *What do I care about here? What matters most?*
- **Gut:** *What feels right or off, beyond explanation?*

Allow a few slow breaths and sense whether these centers feel aligned.

If they feel coherent—calm, grounded, steady—act from that state.

If not, wait. Alignment strengthens when it is given time to settle.

### 4. Leading with Intention

At the start of the day—or before a key meeting—set a simple intention for how you wish to show up.

For example:

*May my actions arise from clarity, courage, and care.*

Choose words that feel alive for you.

This is not about controlling outcomes, but about orienting your inner state. When intention leads, action gains coherence—and results are less likely to compromise who you are.

### 5. Conscious Choice Reflection

At the end of the day, take five minutes to reflect or journal:

- *Where did I choose from awareness today?*
- *Where did I react instead?*
- *What impact did my choices have on others?*
- *What am I learning about how I decide?*

This practice converts experience into discernment. Over time, leadership shifts from habit to authorship.

### 6. The Ripple Practice

Choose one interaction each day and meet it with full presence. Listen, speak, and act as if your state of being will echo beyond the moment.

Afterward, reflect:

- *What did I contribute to the relational field?*
- *What kind of ripple did I create?*

Presence shapes impact. The quality of the moment determines the quality of the ripple.

### 7. The Sacred Interruption

Once or twice a day, interrupt momentum with a single conscious breath.

In that pause, ask:

*What am I creating right now through my state of being?*

Let the question work on you without forcing an answer.

This small return can redirect an entire day.

# CHAPTER 10
# Conscious Creation

*The world as we have created it is a process of our thinking.*
*It cannot be changed without changing our thinking.*
—Albert Einstein

Leadership is often described as decision-making, influence, or execution. Beneath all of these functions lies a more fundamental truth: leadership is always an act of creation.

Every leader, whether consciously or not, is continuously creating—through attention, choices, language, and action. Leaders shape inner states, relationships, cultures, systems, and futures. They create climates of fear or trust, clarity or confusion, meaning or emptiness. They shape what people believe is possible—and what is not.

The central question of leadership, then, is not whether we are creating, but from what level of awareness we create.

Much of what exists in organizations and societies today has been created unconsciously, driven not by deliberate intention but by habit, fear, and compensatory patterns of the ego: the pursuit of status, control, validation, or winning, often at the expense of coherence, meaning, and long-term impact. Even well-intentioned leaders create outcomes they did not foresee and cultures they never consciously chose. The consequences may not be immediate, but they are always real.

Conscious leadership begins when this responsibility is recognized.

At its core, conscious leadership is the **creation of beauty, strength, and love—in us, in others, and out in the world**. This is not a poetic aspiration; it is a guiding principle. Each word is deliberate.

*Beauty* refers to structural harmony—the sense that what is created is aligned with deeper order of life and feels whole and true.

*Strength* refers to clarity, courage, resilience, and the capacity to act and sustain what is created.

*Love* refers to connection, care, and a genuine commitment to dignity, life, and wholeness.

They are foundational qualities that determine whether what we create nurtures or depletes, uplifts or diminishes.

Just as important is the scope of creation implied here. Leaders do not only create outcomes or results. They create themselves through the inner states they cultivate and tolerate. They create others through relational environments in which people either contract or grow. And they create the world through systems and structures that extend far beyond their immediate presence.

Creation without awareness inevitably carries unintended consequences. Strength without love becomes destructive. Love without strength becomes sentimental. Beauty without strength becomes fragile. Conscious leadership does not eliminate these tensions; it learns to hold and integrate them deliberately.

In earlier chapters, we explored conscious breath, listening, coaching, and choice—the inner and relational capacities that make awareness possible. Conscious creation is where those capacities meet the world. It is where intention becomes form, values become structures, and leadership leaves a trace.

This chapter invites a shift in how leadership itself is understood: from managing what exists to taking responsibility for what is being brought into existence.

Once this responsibility is seen, leadership can no longer be reduced to performance or success alone. It becomes a creative and ethical act—one that asks:

*What am I creating?*
*From where am I creating it?*
*And what kind of world does this creation serve?*

## Beauty, Strength, and Love as Design Principles

If conscious leadership is the creation of beauty, strength, and love, then these qualities must be understood not as ideals, but as design principles.

Design principles shape what is built, how it functions, and whether it endures. They are structural, not decorative. In the same way, beauty, strength, and love are not aspirational add-ons to leadership; they quietly determine whether what a leader creates is life-giving or life-depleting, coherent or fragmented, worthy of trust or not.

**Beauty** is the presence of structural harmony. It is the sense that something fits—that values, actions, and outcomes align with one another and with the deeper order they serve. Beauty draws attention back to what is essential. It is often felt as a sense of ease, inspiration, or quiet joy—a natural uplifting of energy that does not need to be forced. It inspires not through demand, but through recognition. In organizations, beauty shows up as clarity of purpose, elegance of process, and environments that integrate rather than fragment. When beauty is absent, systems may still function, but they feel hollow. People comply, but they do not feel connected to why their work matters.

**Strength** is the capacity to act, sustain, and hold under pressure. It includes clarity, courage, resilience, and steadfastness—the ability to stay grounded and break through perceived limitations when it would be easier to pull back. Strength is not force; it is integrity in motion.

In leadership, strength shows up as the capacity to take clear stands, navigate conflict with intention, and follow through with consistency, even under pressure.

Without strength, beauty remains fragile, easily compromised by fear, resistance, or complexity. Leaders who avoid conflict in the name of comfort often create drift, ambiguity, and quiet erosion instead.

**Love** is a commitment to life, to the inherent dignity of people, and to relationships. It is the willingness to see people as whole, not just as roles or functions, even when that reality is inconvenient or complex. It recognizes that we are not separate in the outcomes we create—that what affects one part of the system ultimately affects the whole. In leadership, love shows up as care for impact: who benefits, who bears the cost, and who we are becoming in the process. Without love, strength becomes domination, and beauty becomes superficial. What is created may succeed outwardly while corroding trust and meaning from within.

These three qualities are interdependent. Remove one, and the others lose their integrity. Beauty without strength cannot withstand reality. Strength without love becomes destructive. Love without strength becomes ineffective. Conscious creation does not eliminate the tension between them; it requires learning to hold that tension deliberately.

This is where many leaders struggle—not from ill intent, but from unconsciousness. Driven by compensatory patterns of the ego—the pursuit of status, recognition, control, or winning—leaders often overdevelop one quality at the expense of the others. The result is not outright failure, but miscreation: outcomes that meet goals while quietly undermining meaning, trust, and wholeness.

Consider a company that moves fast and dominates its market. Standards are high. Performance is uncompromising. Results are strong. Yet burnout rises and trust thins. People deliver—but they do not feel valued. Strength is present. Love is not.

Or a company that prioritizes inclusion and psychological safety yet avoids hard conversations and hesitates to uphold standards. Morale improves. Accountability fades. The culture feels kind—but drifts. Love is present. Strength is not.

Or a product built to impress investors with features and speed, yet assembled without architectural coherence. It dazzles at launch but accumulates technical debt and hidden fragility. Beauty is marketed. It is not engineered.

Without integration, what is created fractures eventually — sometimes slowly, sometimes suddenly.

Conscious leadership asks for something more demanding. It asks leaders to design what they create—strategies, organizations, technologies, institutions—with beauty, strength, and love present from the beginning, as guiding forces.

Beauty, strength, and love are not the destination. They are the conditions that determine whether what we create is worth sustaining.

## The Leader as Conscious Creator

Most leadership models implicitly train leaders to become operators.

They emphasize execution, optimization, control, and performance. Leaders are rewarded for efficiency, speed, and measurable outcomes. While these capacities matter, they describe *how* work gets done, not *what kind of world is being created* through it.

A conscious leader understands something deeper: leadership does not merely operate systems; it brings realities into existence.

Through attention, conversations, decisions, and behavior, leaders shape their own inner state and the emotional atmosphere around them long before they shape strategy or structure. They create climates of fear or trust, contraction or possibility. They normalize certain behaviors and marginalize others. Over time, these invisible patterns solidify into culture, systems, and norms that persist long after individual decisions are forgotten.

This is why leadership is never neutral. Even when a leader believes they are "just doing their job," they are actively creating, either consciously or unconsciously. What they tolerate becomes acceptable. What they reward becomes aspirational. What they avoid quietly multiplies.

Creation begins within the leader. The inner state from which a leader operates—reactive or grounded, defended or open, fragmented or coherent—inevitably shapes what follows. Leaders who are disconnected from themselves often create organizations that feel similarly disconnected. Leaders who are internally aligned tend to create environments where clarity and trust are possible. This is a systemic reality. Inner coherence or fragmentation inevitably expresses itself in what is built.[6]

An operator focuses primarily on outputs. A conscious creator pays attention to the source from which action arises. They recognize that beauty, strength, and love cannot be imposed downstream if they are absent upstream—in the way decisions are made, conversations are held, and power is exercised. This shift requires courage.

To lead as a conscious creator means stepping beyond role and identity. It means no longer hiding behind titles, metrics, or inherited playbooks. It means taking responsibility not only for results, but for the human experience those results generate; the level of trust, meaning, vitality, and integrity that surround them.

In this sense, conscious leadership is not about adding new techniques. It is about relating differently to the act of creation itself.

When leaders see themselves as creators rather than operators, a subtle but profound change occurs. Decisions slow just enough to include awareness. Action becomes more intentional. Power becomes stewardship rather than control. And leadership begins to feel less like constant effort and more like aligned participation. From this place, vision does not need to be forced. It begins to emerge.

## Vision as Resonance

When leaders begin to see themselves as creators rather than operators, a familiar question arises: What keeps creation aligned as it unfolds?

Most leadership traditions answer with strategy, ambition, or market opportunity. Vision is treated as a plan—something to be defined, articulated, and executed. While clarity and direction matter, this approach often misses something essential. It produces visions that are logically sound, yet strangely lifeless.

A conscious leader approaches vision differently. At its deepest level, vision is not something a leader fabricates. It is something they recognize. It arises when what matters deeply meets what is genuinely possible. It is felt as coherence between conviction and reality and between what the heart cares about and what the mind knows can be built.

The heart perceives meaning. It knows what matters and what feels alive.

The mind brings discernment. It understands complexity, constraints, and consequences.

When vision arises from only one of these, it becomes distorted.

Heart without mind produces inspiration without direction.

Mind without heart produces efficiency without soul.

Resonant vision integrates both.

This is why compelling visions often feel recognized rather than explained. People sense their coherence before they fully understand them. They feel invited rather than instructed. Vision, in this sense, acts less like a target and more like a pull—quietly organizing attention, effort, and energy toward what wants to come into being.

Leaders who lack this resonance often compensate with force. They rely on incentives, pressure, or persuasion to generate movement. Progress may occur, but it is fragile and costly. Momentum depends on constant reinforcement, while resistance quietly accumulates beneath the surface.

By contrast, when vision is grounded in both conviction and reality, effort becomes more energized and sustainable. Action still requires discipline, but it is animated by meaning rather than compliance. People move not because they are pushed, but because they can feel the direction.

Resonance does not guarantee comfort. Acting in coherence with what truly matters often asks leaders to outgrow familiar identities, abandon outdated goals, or face inconvenient truths. Resonance is not agreement with ego; it is fidelity to what feels true, even when it disrupts existing plans.

For the conscious leader, vision is not a declaration of intent, but an act of listening. It requires the capacity to sit with uncertainty long enough for clarity to emerge and the courage to act from alignment rather than from the need to control.

From this place, creation moves differently. Not faster, but truer. Not louder, but more durable.

Once vision is grounded in resonance, the next question becomes unavoidable: *How does creation unfold without forcing?*

## Creation Without Forcing

When vision is no longer forced or engineered, a different question comes into focus. Not *how do we make this happen*, but what keeps creation aligned as it unfolds.

The instinct to force is deeply ingrained in leadership. Pressure, urgency, and control are often mistaken for effectiveness. Yet much of what leaders struggle with—resistance, burnout, brittle systems—arises not from a lack of effort, but from effort applied at the wrong level.

Conscious creation operates by a different principle.

Rather than imposing form from the outside, it relies on attunement—the capacity to remain in relationship with what is emerging and to respond from awareness rather than impulse. This does not mean passivity. It requires presence, discernment, and the courage to act when the moment calls for it. But action arises from listening, not forcing.

Imagination plays a central role here. In conscious leadership, imagination is not fantasy or wishful thinking. It is a perceptive faculty; the ability to sense possibilities that are not yet fully formed. Imagination allows leaders to feel into future impact, to recognize potential before it is visible, and to hold space for what wants to come into being.[7] When imagination is suppressed, creation collapses into repetition. Leaders recycle familiar patterns because they can no longer sense alternatives. When imagination is paired with attunement, flow becomes possible.

Flow is not a state to be chased, nor a peak performance trick. It emerges naturally when intention, effort, and timing align. In flow, action feels neither rushed nor stalled. There is effort, but not strain, and action arises with a quality of effortless effort.[5] Movement unfolds without constant self-correction because attention is anchored in the present moment rather than anxiously projected toward outcomes.

Leaders often block flow by over-controlling timing and acting too early out of fear, or too late out of hesitation. Creation without forcing requires the discipline to wait as much as the courage to act. It asks leaders to trust coherence over urgency.[8]

As ego relaxes, another shift occurs: creation reveals itself as co-creation.

No meaningful creation happens in isolation. Leaders create with people, systems, constraints, and contexts that have their own intelligence and momentum. Even circumstances that appear limiting often carry information about what is possible now. When leaders treat these forces as obstacles to overcome, they exhaust themselves and those around them. When they treat them as participants in the creative process, something opens.

Co-creation does not diminish leadership authority; it refines it. Power shifts from control to stewardship. Listening becomes a creative act. Humility becomes a form of strength. The leader's role is no longer to dictate outcomes, but to engage in creative collaboration—staying aligned while enabling emergence.

This way of creating feels unfamiliar to leaders trained in command-and-control environments. It can feel risky, even irresponsible. Yet over time, it proves more resilient. What emerges through attunement tends to endure because it is shaped in relationship with reality rather than imposed upon it.

Creation without forcing does not guarantee ease. It often demands patience, restraint, and the willingness to remain in uncertainty longer than is comfortable. But it reduces the hidden costs of miscreation that include burnout, resistance, and unintended harm. When leaders stop trying to force the future, they begin to participate consciously in its unfolding.

## Ferocity Rooted in Awareness

It is important to name a common misunderstanding of conscious creation.

Many people hear words like awareness, presence, and attunement and assume that conscious leadership is gentle, slow, or accommodating; that it avoids urgency, sharp decisions, or disruptive force. This could not be further from the truth.

Creation, at its highest levels, often demands ferocity. It requires a clear inner vision, relentless commitment to excellence, and the willingness to move decisively in the face of resistance. True creation disrupts what already exists. It dismantles what no longer works. It removes obstacles—sometimes including ineffective structures, outdated strategies, and people who are no longer aligned with what must be built. It does not wait for consensus when clarity is present.

The presence of consciousness does not negate this fire. It determines its source.

There is a critical difference between ego-driven ferocity and ferocity rooted in awareness.

Ego-driven ferocity is compensatory. It arises from an inner sense of lack and attempts to fill it through domination, urgency, or achievement. It is fueled by fear: the fear of falling behind, of being insignificant, of losing control, or of being exposed. This form of drive often justifies harm in the name of urgency or greatness. People become expendable. Relationships are sacrificed. The mission becomes a shield for unresolved insecurity. Results may be achieved, but trust erodes, dignity collapses, and long-term coherence is damaged.

Ferocity rooted in awareness is different. It does not arise from fear, but from clarity. Not from proving, but from commitment. Not from insecurity, but from devotion to what must be created.

This kind of ferocity is grounded, not frantic. Decisive, not reactive. It can move fast without losing integrity, cut cleanly without cruelty, and disrupt the status quo without collapsing into chaos. It is willing to make hard calls, including releasing people, ending initiatives, and dismantling structures that no longer serve, without collapsing into righteousness or justification. These decisions are not driven by image or impulse, but by responsibility to the whole.

Awareness refines and purifies resolve. When ferocity is rooted in awareness, urgency becomes precise rather than panicked. Focus becomes unwavering rather than obsessive. Standards remain uncompromising without becoming dehumanizing. The leader does not mistake intensity for strength or speed for wisdom. They know when to push, when to pause, when to destroy what is obsolete, and when to protect what is essential.

This is strength integrated with love. Fire guided by intelligence. Power aligned with purpose.

Conscious creation does not ask leaders to soften their edge. It asks them to sharpen it without letting it be driven by compensation, fear, or egoic hunger.

The question is not whether you are willing to act decisively. The question is: *What is driving that decisiveness?*

When ferocity arises from awareness rather than insecurity, creation gains endurance. What is built can last—not because it was forced into existence, but because it was built with clarity, courage, and care for what it must sustain over time. This is the ferocity conscious leadership requires.

## Envisioning Impact Before Outcome

Much of modern leadership is trained to fixate on outcomes.

Targets are defined, metrics are set, and success is measured by whether predetermined goals are achieved. This orientation is efficient, but it carries a hidden cost. When leaders focus narrowly on outcomes, they often fail to consider the impact those outcomes will have on people, culture, and the future that unfolds from them.

Conscious creation reverses this sequence. Rather than asking first, *What do we want to achieve?* Consciousleaders begin with a deeper inquiry:

*What kind of impact will this creation have—on human beings, on systems, and on the world it enters?*

Impact precedes outcome because outcomes are temporary, while impact endures. An initiative may hit its numbers and still erode trust. A strategy may win the market and still exhaust the people who carried it. A technological breakthrough may optimize efficiency while quietly diminishing agency, dignity, or meaning. When impact is not consciously envisioned, outcomes can succeed while creation fails.

Envisioning impact before outcome does not slow leadership down. It refines it. It asks leaders to sense forward into the life of what they are creating—to imagine how it will shape behavior, identity, and possibility long after the initial result is achieved. This is where imagination becomes a moral faculty.

In conscious leadership, imagination is not fantasy or aspiration. It is the capacity to feel into consequences before they materialize, to perceive second- and third-order effects, and to recognize whether what is being created will strengthen or weaken the fabric of life around it.

When leaders envision impact first, beauty, strength, and love are no longer abstract principles. They become essential ingredients of creation.

The question is no longer only, *Can this work?*

It becomes: *What will this create—in us, in others, and in the world over time?*

I once worked with a CEO who came to me energized by a bold strategic initiative. The numbers were compelling, the timeline aggressive, and the board enthusiastic. On paper, it was a clear win.

As he described the plan, there was intensity in his voice—sharp focus, relentless drive. It was impressive. And yet something felt off. His pace was fast, his breath shallow, his energy tight. There was urgency, but no sense of inner stability.

At a natural pause, I asked a simple question:

"What's really driving this?"

He answered without hesitation: market pressure, competition, the need to stay ahead. Then I asked another question, more slowly:

"And if this didn't work—what would it mean to you?"

He stopped. I noticed the familiar urge to fill the silence—and chose not to.

After a long moment, he spoke more quietly. Beneath the strategic rationale was something more personal: a fear of falling behind, a need to prove relevance, an unspoken belief that slowing down would be seen as weakness.

The initiative wasn't just about growth. It was a compensatory act of the ego—an attempt to outrun uncertainty rather than meet it. Nothing about this made him a bad leader. It made him a human one.

As the conversation continued, something softened. The urgency eased. His breathing slowed. And a different question emerged—not from fear, but from presence:

*What am I actually trying to create here?*

That question changed everything.

Over the weeks that followed, the strategy evolved. The ambition remained, but the source shifted. The work was no longer fueled by comparison or pressure, but by a clearer sense of purpose. Leadership capacity was strengthened rather than stretched thin. Success was no longer measured only by speed and scale, but by the depth of commitment and alignment the vision inspired.

The initiative succeeded, and the organization was stronger for it.

This time, it emerged from alignment rather than compensation.

What changed was not the intelligence of the plan.

What changed was the source of creation.

When creation moves from ego to essence—from proving to serving—it becomes not only more effective, but more humane.

## TAKEAWAYS

- Leadership is always an act of creation.

  Whether consciously or unconsciously, leaders shape people, cultures, and futures through what they bring into being—through attention, choices, language, and presence.

- Outcomes can succeed while impact quietly fails.

  Conscious creation begins by envisioning what a decision will shape over time, not only what it will achieve in the short term.

- Ego-driven creation is fueled by compensation, not clarity.

  When leadership is driven by fear, comparison, or the need to prove relevance, it can generate results while eroding trust, vitality, dignity, and long-term coherence.

- Conscious creation does not eliminate ferocity—it refines it.

  Awareness does not weaken resolve; it purifies its source. Creation often requires urgency, decisive action, and the courage to dismantle what no longer serves, but when ferocity is rooted in awareness rather than ego, it creates strength without cruelty and change without losing integrity.

- Creation rooted in alignment produces strength without force.

  When intention, awareness, and action are coherent, leaders mobilize commitment and collaboration rather than pressure and compliance.

- Imagination is a moral faculty of leadership.

  It allows leaders to sense consequences before they materialize and to act responsibly within complexity rather than reacting from habit or fear.

- In an age of AI, tools amplify the consciousness that guides them.

  Without inner orientation, increased capability leads to dependence and harm; with awareness, it becomes an instrument of stewardship and wisdom.

- Conscious creation asks a different question.

  Not only Can this work? but What will this create—in us, in others, and in the world it shapes over time?

## PRACTICES

These practices are designed to help you recognize when creation is being driven by ego or fear and to re-source action from awareness and alignment—without losing momentum, urgency, or resolve.

They are not about doing less. They are about creating from the right source.

### 1. Pause at the Moment of Urgency

Bring this practice into moments when:

- a decision feels pressing
- stakes feel high
- speed or certainty is being rewarded

Pause—not to stop action, but to slow the source of action.

Take one deliberate breath. Let your attention settle into the body.

Urgency remains—but it becomes directed rather than reactive.

### 2. Sense the Source

Without analyzing, ask yourself quietly:

- *What is driving this impulse to act right now?*
- *Is it fear, comparison, pressure, or the need to prove something?*
- *Or is it clarity, commitment, and devotion to what truly matters here?*

You are not looking for a "better" answer—only an honest one.

Awareness does not weaken action. It purifies it.

### 3. Envision Impact Before Outcome

Before deciding what to do, sense forward into what this choice will shape.

Ask:

- *What will this create in me as a leader?*
- *What will it create in the people involved?*
- *What kind of culture, system, or future will this reinforce over time?*

Let images, sensations, or felt responses arise.

This is imagination as discernment, not fantasy.

When impact is envisioned early, unintended harm becomes less likely.

### 4. Re-Choose the Action

Now ask:

- *What action would I take if this were sourced from awareness rather than fear?*
- *What would strength look like here—without force?*
- *What decision serves life, not image?*

Act from that place. The external decision may look similar. What changes is the source from which it is carried forward.

### 5. Notice the Difference

After acting, notice:

- the quality of engagement that follows
- the level of ownership or resistance
- your own inner state

This feedback is often more revealing than outcomes alone.

Creation teaches in real time—if you are willing to listen.

**6. Release to Create**

Conscious creation is not only about building. It is also about ending what has completed its purpose.

Before something new can emerge, something old often must be released.

Pause and ask:

- *What is no longer alive or serving its purpose?*
- *What am I holding onto out of habit, fear, or attachment rather than truth?*
- *What would become possible if this were cleanly let go?*

Notice any contraction when you imagine release. That contraction often signals attachment—not necessity.

If release is required, act decisively and cleanly. Avoid dragging out endings with hesitation or justification. Lingering often causes more harm than clarity.

Destruction rooted in awareness is precise rather than reactive. It clears space without blame and ends without contempt.

Creation requires courage not only to build, but to release what has completed its work.

CHAPTER 11

# Conscious Healing

*The wound is the place where the light enters you.*

–Rumi

The higher purpose of any relationship is to help each other heal and evolve. Leadership is often described in terms of vision, execution, and results. Rarely is it described in terms of healing. And yet, wherever humans gather to work, create, and decide together, pain is inevitably present. Fear, mistrust, unresolved conflict, and wounds carried forward from past experiences, past leaders, and even past generations.

The question is not whether leaders will encounter pain. The question is whether they will transmit it—or transform it.

Unconscious leadership tends to transmit pain forward. Pressure spreads pressure. Fear creates fear. Unexamined wounds quietly shape decisions, cultures, and outcomes. Often, unintentionally, leaders pass on what they themselves have not yet resolved.

Conscious leadership interrupts this cycle.

A conscious leader recognizes that leadership is not exercised from outside the system. Leaders are *within* the field they influence. Their inner state—regulated or reactive, grounded or fearful—becomes part of the emotional, psychological, and relational atmosphere of the organization.

This is where healing enters leadership, not as therapy, and not as sentimentality, but as responsibility.

Those who cause pain often carry pain within. When inner wounds remain unseen, they tend to express themselves through control, blame, urgency, or withdrawal. What appears as a leadership style is often an unexamined survival strategy.

Healing begins when leaders are willing to turn inward—to become aware of what they are carrying. This inner work is not self-indulgent. It is necessary because what leaders carry inevitably spills into others. Leaders who do not attend to their own wounds will eventually ask others to carry them instead.

From this perspective, healing is not about eliminating difficulty or avoiding conflict. It is about restoring wholeness, coherence, and flow—within oneself, between people, and across systems.

As leadership extends beyond individuals into teams, organizations, and societies, the implications deepen. Organizations carry their own histories—unresolved tensions, unspoken fears, cultural trauma. Entire industries and institutions operate inside inherited narratives shaped by scarcity, domination, and mistrust.

At a civilizational level, leadership is unfolding amid unprecedented amplification. Artificial intelligence does not introduce new values into the world; it magnifies the consciousness already at work. Unhealed systems, when scaled by powerful technologies, become more potent.

In this context, conscious leadership is no longer only about performance or success. It is about whether leadership becomes a force for healing or a mechanism for accelerating harm.

This chapter explores what it means to lead as a conscious healer, beginning with the self, extending into relationships, and ultimately shaping organizations and the future we are collectively creating.

The Inner Work of the Leader

Every leader brings more into a room than a title or a set of skills. They bring their inner state. Their nervous system. Their unexamined beliefs. Their unresolved experiences and traumas.[9]

Leadership is never neutral. It transmits the inner state of the leader into the system. It is energetic, emotional, and psychological. What has not been integrated within the leader will inevitably express itself through their decisions, tone, and presence.

Unhealed fear often shows up as control. Unhealed shame becomes blame or withdrawal. Unprocessed trauma expresses itself as reactivity, hypervigilance, or rigidity.[10]

These patterns are rarely conscious. They often masquerade as efficiency, high standards, or decisiveness. Yet beneath them lies a simple truth: what has not been healed within seeks expression without.

Healing begins when leaders are willing to turn toward themselves—to see clearly. To recognize the moments when their reactions are disproportionate, their certainty defensive, or their urgency compulsive.

This inner work requires the capacity to sit with discomfort. To feel fear without acting from it. To notice contraction without immediately trying to eliminate it. Leaders who lack this capacity often externalize discomfort through pressure, micromanagement, or emotional distance.

Self-healing is the gradual removal of distortion from perception and choice. As leaders become more regulated and self-aware, their responses become more deliberate. Their listening deepens. Their actions arise from clarity rather than compulsion.

This work is taking responsibility for what one carries. As leaders tend to their inner life, they reduce the unconscious burden placed on others. They no longer burden their teams with unprocessed anxiety, fear, or unspoken expectations.

In this way, healing within becomes a form of inner stewardship—tending the inner field so it doesn't spill unconsciously into others. It restores coherence to the system at its source. Only from this ground can healing in relationship and healing in organizations genuinely occur.

## Relational Healing

Leadership does not happen in isolation. It happens in relationship—through conversations, conflicts, expectations, disappointments, and moments of trust. Every interaction becomes a potential site of either healing or harm. From this perspective, healing emerges when a leader creates the conditions for growth rather than attempting to fix it.

One of the most common leadership misunderstandings is the belief that to help someone is to fix them. Advice is offered quickly. Solutions are provided before understanding has fully emerged. Responsibility is quietly taken away in the name of support.

Yet fixing, even when well-intended, often communicates a subtle message: *You are not capable on your own.*[11] Healing in relationship begins when leaders relinquish the need to rescue.

The higher purpose of any relationship is mutual healing and evolution—not mere comfort or agreement. It requires the courage to engage difficulty in ways that preserve dignity, agency, and truth.

Conscious leaders create relational conditions for healing by offering presence without judgment, compassion without taking over, accountability without shame, and support without substitution. These conditions require restraint. It is often harder to stay present than to intervene. Harder to listen than to advise. Harder to trust another's capacity than to impose one's own.

Relational healing also requires clear boundaries. Compassion does not mean absorbing another's emotions. Empathy does not mean excusing behavior. Conscious leaders learn to distinguish between understanding someone's pain and carrying their responsibility for them. Healing restores agency—it does not replace it.

When leaders genuinely trust others' capacity, something fundamental changes in the relationship. People begin to access their own intelligence. Difficult conversations become possible. Mistakes become teachers rather than threats. Growth emerges not because it is forced, but because it is safe.

In this way, relationships become developmental fields, the spaces where pain is met consciously, integrated, and transformed. As these relational patterns repeat across teams, they begin to shape culture. What is practiced between two people becomes normalized within the system.

Healing, then, is not confined to one conversation or one relationship. It shapes the culture that forms around it.

## Healing Organizations

Organizations, like individuals, carry history. Decisions made under pressure, conflicts left unresolved, values compromised for survival, voices silenced over time—none of this simply disappears. It accumulates.

What often shows up as performance issues, disengagement, resistance to change, or internal politics is rarely just about strategy or competence. More often, these are symptoms of unresolved organizational wounds.

Every organization has its blockages—places where energy no longer flows freely. Knots formed through repeated conflict. Inhibitions created by fear, punishment, or broken trust. Over time, these patterns become normalized. "That's just how things are done here."

Leaders who approach organizations purely as machines tend to respond with structural fixes—reorganizations, new metrics, new incentives, new processes—or by changing the people themselves through cycles of firing and hiring. While these tools have their place, they cannot heal what is fundamentally relational and emotional in nature.

Healing organizations require leaders to see systems as living fields of relationships. This means learning to recognize when a system is dysregulated, when reactivity replaces clarity, when compliance replaces commitment, when silence replaces honesty. It means understanding that cultures often protect their wounds by resisting precisely what would heal them. The work of the conscious leader is not to force change, but to restore coherence.

This often begins by naming what has been unspoken. Acknowledging past harms. Allowing difficult truths to surface without retaliation. Creating conditions where people feel safe enough to be honest and strong enough to be accountable.[12]

Healing does not mean avoiding hard truths or preserving harmony at all costs. In organizations, healing often begins by clearly identifying the underlying issue, whether it is a pattern of mistrust, a breach of values, or behavior that is no longer tolerable. Sometimes healing requires firm boundaries. Sometimes it requires forgiveness. And sometimes it requires letting go of a "bad apple" whose presence continues to poison the system.

These decisions are rarely simple. They demand discernment rather than rules, and courage rather than certainty. A conscious leader does not confuse compassion with tolerance of harm, nor healing with indefinite accommodation. True healing restores integrity to the system—even when doing so is uncomfortable or costly.

Organizational healing does not happen overnight. It unfolds gradually as trust is rebuilt, as patterns are interrupted, and as people experience consistency between words and actions. Over time, what was blocked begins to move. What was inhibited begins to express. What was knotted begins to loosen.

In this way, healing becomes a form of organizational renewal, thus restoring flow to the system itself.

## Systemic Healing

Leadership does not occur in a vacuum. Every organization, industry, and institution operates within larger historical, cultural, and civilizational contexts. These contexts carry unresolved trauma—between nations, between races, between ideologies, and between ways of seeing the world.

Much of what shows up in modern organizations—mistrust, polarization, fear-based decision-making, short-term thinking—cannot be fully understood at the individual level alone. These patterns are inherited. They are shaped by histories of domination, scarcity, exclusion, and unresolved collective pain.

In this sense, leaders today inherit more than strategies and structures. They inherit unfinished histories. When these systemic wounds remain unseen, they quietly shape behavior. "Us versus them" thinking becomes normalized. Control masquerades as competence. Efficiency overrides empathy. Organizations begin to mirror the fractures of the broader culture rather than transcend them.

The role of the conscious leader at this level is not to solve civilizational trauma—that would be neither realistic nor appropriate. But it *is* to recognize when pain is systemic rather than personal, and to resist the impulse to collapse complex collective wounds into individual blame.

This responsibility becomes more pronounced in the age of artificial intelligence.

Technologies now scale not only intelligence, but also distortion.

When fear, mistrust, or unexamined bias remain unresolved within leaders and systems, amplification accelerates their consequences.[13] In this context, conscious leadership becomes a form of civilizational stewardship.

Leaders who have not engaged their own inner work—who have not learned to heal relational and organizational wounds—are far more likely to perpetuate and transmit inherited patterns, now magnified by powerful technologies. Conversely, leaders who can hold complexity, tolerate discomfort, and act from clarity rather than fear become stabilizing forces in an accelerating world.

Systemic healing does not begin with grand solutions. It begins with awareness of scale. With humility about what leadership can shape and what it cannot control. With a commitment to stop carrying forward unexamined historical pain into the systems now being built.

This is how healing at the civilizational level quietly begins, not through ideology or control, but through consciousness expressed in leadership.

## The Leader as Healer

At every level—self, relationship, organization, and system—healing ultimately comes down to the leader's stance. Healing leadership begins as a way of being.

The conscious healer is not a fixer. Fixing assumes something is broken and needs to be corrected from the outside. It places the leader above the system, armed with answers. While this approach can produce short-term results, it often creates long-term dependency, resentment, or fragility.

Nor is the conscious healer a savior. Saving removes agency. It subtly communicates that others cannot be trusted with their own growth, responsibility, or capacity. Over time, this erodes strength rather than building it.

The conscious healer leads from a different stance. They trust that beneath confusion, conflict, or dysfunction, there is an underlying intelligence-seeking expression. Their work is not to impose solutions, but to create the conditions in which that intelligence can surface.

This stance requires strength rooted in clarity and courage. Clarity to see what is actually happening, rather than what is convenient to see. Courage to remain present when others are uncomfortable, emotional, or uncertain. Courage to hold boundaries without hardening, and compassion without collapsing.

The leader as healer is willing to stand in tension. To resist premature resolution. To allow complexity to unfold long enough for deeper understanding to emerge.

Importantly, this stance does not exempt leaders from making hard decisions. On the contrary, it demands more responsibility. Decisions made from clarity rather than fear tend to be firmer, fairer, and more enduring.

When leaders operate from this place, healing is no longer an intervention. It becomes a byproduct of how leadership is exercised. People feel seen without being managed. Held without being controlled. Challenged without being diminished.

In this way, the leader does not "heal" others. They stop interfering with the natural capacity for healing that already exists within people and systems. Over time, leadership exercised from this stance reshapes the system itself. People grow stronger rather than dependent. Trust deepens rather than erodes. What once required intervention begins to regulate itself.

When Maya stepped into the CEO role, she inherited a company that looked functional from the outside and exhausted from within. Results were acceptable. People were polite. Meetings were orderly and controlled. And yet, turnover was quietly rising, decisions stalled, and trust felt thin.

Her first instinct was familiar. Diagnose the problems. Restructure the teams. Replace a few leaders who were "no longer a fit." She had done this before, successfully. But something gave her pause. Instead of acting immediately, she began by listening.

Not performative listening. Real listening. One-on-ones

without agendas. Meetings where silence was allowed. Questions were asked without offering immediate answers. What emerged was not incompetence, but fatigue. Not resistance, but fear. People spoke of past leaders who had moved fast, punished mistakes, and left little room for dissent.

Maya recognized something uncomfortable. The urgency she felt to "fix" the organization was the same urgency she had learned to carry earlier in her career—an inherited pattern equating control with competence. She realized that before changing the system, she had to change how she showed up within it. She slowed herself first.

She noticed when her body tightened in meetings, when impatience disguised itself as decisiveness. When certainty became a defense. Instead of acting on those impulses, she named them internally and chose differently. Her presence softened. Her tone changed. Her listening deepened. Something shifted.

Conversations became more honest. Conflict surfaced—not explosively, but clearly. Longstanding tensions between teams were finally named. A senior leader who had been quietly undermining trust was addressed directly. After several attempts at repair, Maya made the difficult decision to let him go. The relief in the system was immediate.

At the same time, she modeled forgiveness where appropriate. Past mistakes were acknowledged without blame. Trust was rebuilt through consistency rather than promises. Over time, people stopped waiting for permission and started taking ownership again.

The organization did not transform overnight. But it began to regulate itself. Decisions moved faster without pressure. Feedback became more direct without hostility. Energy returned, though not through incentives, but through restored integrity.

What changed was more than strategy. The field itself shifted.

Maya healed the organization by interrupting the transmission of fear. She did so first within herself, then in a relationship, and eventually across the system.

The impact extended beyond the company. As new technologies were adopted and AI systems introduced, decisions were made with more care, more inclusion, and more foresight. The organization became less reactive, more thoughtful—less driven by fear disguised as urgency, more guided by conscious choice.

This is how healing scales in leadership. Quietly. Relationally. Systemically.

## TAKEAWAYS

- Healing is inseparable from leadership.

  Wherever people work together, unresolved pain will either be transmitted unconsciously or met consciously. Leadership determines whether fear spreads—or coherence is restored.

- Healing begins within the leader.

  What remains unexamined within a leader will shape decisions, tone, and culture. Inner work reduces the unconscious burden placed on others.

- Relational healing restores agency.

  Healing in relationship is not fixing or rescuing. It emerges when leaders hold accountability without shame, offer presence without taking over, and trust others' capacity to grow.

- Organizations carry history.

  Many performance issues are symptoms of unresolved relational wounds. Structural solutions alone cannot repair what is fundamentally emotional and cultural.

- Healing requires clarity and boundaries.

  Compassion is not tolerance of harm. Restoring integrity may require difficult conversations, firm limits, forgiveness, or clean endings.

- At scale, consciousness is amplified.

  In an age of powerful technologies, especially AI, unexamined patterns spread faster and further. Awareness determines whether leadership accelerates harm or deepens responsibility.

- The leader as healer is a steward, not a savior.

  Healing does not come from control or intervention, but from presence, clarity, and responsibility. Over time, this stance strengthens people, restores trust, and allows systems to regulate themselves.

## PRACTICES

These practices invite you to notice what is present—what is driving action, what is ready to be seen more clearly, and what is ready to be healed or resolved.

They are most powerful when brought into real moments, especially when something feels charged, uncertain, or unresolved.

### 1. Inner Stewardship in Real Time

Notice moments when urgency, irritation, defensiveness, or the impulse to fix arises.

Pause just long enough to ask:

*What am I carrying right now that may shape how I respond?*

Feel it in the body before acting. This practice shifts action from reaction to responsibility. Over time, it reduces the unconscious transmission of fear, pressure, or reactivity into others.

### 2. Relating to Others as Capable

In your next challenging interaction, resist the urge to advise, rescue, or solve too quickly.

Listen fully. Reflect what you hear. Allow space. Then ask yourself:

*What becomes possible if I fully trust this person's capacity to think, choose, and respond?*

Notice how the quality of the relationship changes when you stop carrying what belongs to the other.

### 3. Naming the Real Issue

When a pattern persists in your team or organization, pause before applying another structural solution. Ask yourself:

*What real issue are we avoiding? What has gone unnamed?*

It may be a breakdown of trust, a misalignment of values, a tolerated behavior, or an unresolved conflict. Healing often begins with honest naming.

### 4. Boundaries as a Healing Act

Reflect on one situation where compassion may be sliding into accommodation.

Ask:

*What boundary would restore integrity here?*

Clear expectations, consequences, or even a clean ending can restore coherence. When exercised from clarity rather than anger, boundaries strengthen trust rather than fracture it.

### 5. Interrupting Transmission

Consider the systems, teams, or technologies you are shaping. Ask yourself:

*What patterns am I carrying forward, and which ones must stop with me?*

Leadership at scale amplifies what is unresolved. This practice reinforces leadership as stewardship of the future—not merely management of the present.

CHAPTER 12

# Conscious Transformation

*Try not to resist the changes that come your way.*
*Instead, let life live through you.*
—Rumi

Transformation is often misunderstood as improvement, whether it's becoming more skilled, more efficient, or more capable within an existing identity. But conscious transformation is something else entirely. It is not an upgrade to the current self. It is a crossing of a threshold.[14]

At moments of true transformation, what is required is not addition, but release. Old identities loosen. Familiar ways of knowing lose their authority. The strategies that once brought success no longer produce coherence. What worked before begins to constrain what wants to emerge next.

This is why transformation is rarely comfortable. It involves letting go before there is clarity about what comes next.[15] It asks leaders to remain present as certainty dissolves and direction has not yet re-formed. In this in-between space, many attempt to restore control by returning to familiar patterns. Others rush to replace one identity with another. Both moves short-circuit transformation.

Conscious transformation requires a different posture: openness rather than resistance, curiosity rather than control, trust rather than premature certainty. It is the willingness to allow something to end so that something new can be born.

This pattern—death and rebirth—is the lived structure of transformation. Roles, beliefs, and self-concepts dissolve before new capacities stabilize. The leader reorganizes at a deeper level, in alignment with emerging truth.

For leaders, this matters now more than ever. We are living in a period of accelerating change where existing maps no longer reliably describe the terrain.[16] Technologies such as artificial intelligence, biotechnology, and planetary-scale communication networks are amplifying speed, complexity, and consequence. In this environment, leadership rooted in fixed identity and control-based certainty becomes brittle.

Conscious transformation is the capacity to remain grounded while crossing into the unknown, to let go of what no longer fits, to stay present through disorientation, and to allow new ways of seeing, choosing, and creating to emerge.

This chapter explores transformation not as a dramatic event, but as a disciplined passage. A movement from what has been, through what must end, into what has not yet taken form.

## Letting Go: The First Act of Transformation

Every genuine transformation begins with letting go. It is the first act of transformation; an initiation into what must change.

Before something new can emerge, something old must loosen its grip. Identities that once provided stability begin to feel constraining. Assumptions that once felt reliable no longer hold. Ways of leading that previously produced results start to generate friction instead of flow.

For leaders, this moment is often confusing. What is being asked to end may not be broken. It may have worked exceptionally well. Letting go, then, arises when something has fulfilled its purpose, even if it is still working.

This is why letting go is so difficult. It threatens the very sources of competence, confidence, and recognition that leaders have relied on. Control, certainty, and expertise are not easily surrendered, especially in environments that reward decisiveness and predictability.

Yet transformation does not negotiate with attachment. As long as leaders cling to familiar identities or methods, they remain anchored to the past—even while trying to create the future. What is held too tightly cannot evolve. What is defended cannot transform.

Letting go requires discernment. It asks leaders to recognize when their effort no longer creates movement, but merely sustains what already exists—when clarity tightens into control.

This phase often feels like loss. Not only of roles or strategies, but of certainty itself. Leaders may experience a temporary loss of direction, authority, or confidence. This is not a sign that transformation has gone wrong. It is a sign that it has begun.

Those who cannot tolerate this discomfort often rush to replace what is ending with something familiar—new structures, new labels, new strategies that preserve the old identity in different form. In doing so, they interrupt the deeper process that transformation requires.

Surrender is the countermovement to this impulse. Not surrender as giving up, but surrender as allowing. It is the willingness to stop forcing resolution and to trust the process of emergence itself. In leadership, surrender is the willingness to release control over outcomes that can no longer be shaped from who you used to be.

This kind of surrender requires strength. It asks leaders to stay present without grasping, to remain engaged without dictating form, and to allow uncertainty without retreat. What looks like inaction from the outside is often a deeper form of participation—one that makes space for something genuinely new to arise.

Letting go creates space. And space, while uncomfortable, is the necessary condition for emergence. Only by releasing what no longer fits can leaders make room for what has not yet taken shape.

## Death and Rebirth

Every genuine transformation follows a pattern that is rarely named and often resisted: death and rebirth.

This is not a metaphor meant to dramatize change. It describes a lived process in which an old way of being dissolves before a new one can take form. Identities, roles, beliefs, and sources of authority that once defined the leader lose their coherence. What once felt solid no longer does.

For many leaders, this phase is the most unsettling. The old no longer works, but the new is not yet available. Familiar reference points disappear. Confidence wavers. The question *Who am I now?* arises viscerally—an embodied rupture rather than a conceptual inquiry.

This in-between phase is often misread as failure or regression. In reality, it is a necessary passage. Just as in nature, transformation requires breakdown before reorganization. What is dying must be allowed to complete its cycle so that something new can be born.

The discomfort of this phase tempts leaders to escape it. Some rush to resurrect the old identity by reasserting authority or doubling down on control. Others prematurely adopt a new persona or philosophy, bypassing the deeper work of transformation. Both moves interrupt the process and leave the underlying shift incomplete.

Death, in this context, is not the loss of capability. It is the loosening of identification.

What is often dissolving at this stage is the ego—not as arrogance or selfishness, but as the psychological structure that once organized identity, safety, and control. The ego develops to protect, to create coherence, and to help leaders succeed within known terrain. But what protects at one stage can constrain at the next.

Transformation therefore requires a loosening of the ego's grip—not its elimination, but the release of its need to dominate perception, decision-making, and self-definition. As these protective strategies soften, leaders experience both vulnerability and relief. What falls away is the strain of self-protection. Capacity remains freer, less defended, and more available.

Rebirth does not arrive on command. It emerges gradually, often quietly, as new orientations begin to stabilize. Leaders notice subtle shifts in how they perceive situations, relate to others, and make decisions. What once required effort begins to feel natural. What once felt threatening becomes workable.

Importantly, rebirth does not restore the leader to who they were before. There is no return to the old normal. What emerges is a different way of inhabiting leadership that is less defended, less performative, and more grounded.

Leaders who allow this process to unfold often discover that what first felt like loss was actually the shedding of what confined them. By releasing what had to end, they gain access to new capacities, perspectives, and possibilities that were previously unavailable.

Death and rebirth recur throughout a leader's evolution. Each threshold crossed expands what is possible—not only for the leader, but for the systems they influence.

## Embracing the Unknown

After letting go and the dissolution of the old, leaders find themselves in unfamiliar territory. The reference points that once guided action no longer apply, yet new ones have not fully formed. This is the space of the unknown.

Most leadership training is designed to minimize time spent here. Leaders are taught to reduce uncertainty, clarify direction, and restore predictability as quickly as possible. But in moments of true transformation, the unknown cannot be eliminated without aborting the process itself.

The unknown is not a problem to solve. It is the condition in which new possibilities can emerge.

For leaders accustomed to certainty and control, this space is deeply uncomfortable. The impulse is to act—to decide, to declare, to impose direction. Action restores a sense of agency, even when it is premature. But in the context of transformation, premature certainty often recreates the past rather than opening the future.

Embracing the unknown requires a different capacity. It asks leaders to remain present without answers, to hold tension without resolution, and to resist collapsing complexity into false clarity. This stance reflects disciplined patience in service of emergence.

In this space, leadership shifts from prediction to sensing. Instead of asking, "What should we do?" leaders begin asking, "What is trying to emerge?" Attention moves from controlling outcomes to listening—listening for subtle signals of readiness, coherence, and alignment within themselves and the systems they lead.

This way of leading cannot be rushed. The unknown reveals itself incrementally through observation, dialogue, and small, responsive experiments. Leaders learn to move in shorter arcs—acting, sensing, adjusting—guided less by certainty and more by coherence.

Importantly, embracing the unknown does not mean abandoning responsibility. Decisions are still made. Direction is still given. But action is sourced from presence rather than fear, from awareness rather than habit. Over time, this builds trust—internally and relationally—because leadership feels grounded rather than reactive.

Leaders who can stay with the unknown without grasping discover a quieter form of confidence. Not the confidence of knowing what will happen, but the confidence of being able to meet whatever unfolds. This capacity becomes essential in environments shaped by accelerating change, where no map remains reliable for long.

Embracing the unknown is more than a phase to pass through. It becomes a leadership stance, one that creates space not only for personal transformation but also for futures that could not have been planned in advance.

## Metamorphosis

Transformation reaches a decisive point when letting go, dissolution, and not-knowing begin to reorganize who the leader is. This is metamorphosis.

Metamorphosis is not improvement. It is not adding new skills to an existing identity. It is a fundamental reconfiguration: an irreversible shift in how a leader perceives, relates, and acts. Just as in nature, the old form does not gradually evolve into the new. It dissolves, and something different takes shape.

This phase can feel disorienting. Leaders may find that familiar competencies no longer function as they once did, while new capacities are not yet fully reliable. What once brought authority now feels insufficient. What once felt like mastery gives way to humility.

From the outside, this stage can look like regression or loss of edge. From the inside, it often feels like vulnerability mixed with clarity. Leaders are no longer performing from habit or identity but responding from presence. Action becomes less driven, yet more intentional.

Metamorphosis requires tolerance for this temporary loss of form. Leaders must remain engaged even when they no longer feel like experts, when certainty has not yet returned, and when external validation is scarce. What looks like incompetence is often the necessary instability that precedes reorganization.

As the transformation stabilizes, leaders begin to notice subtle but profound shifts. Decisions arise from a deeper place. Listening becomes more spacious. Action feels less reactive and more aligned. Effort decreases even as impact increases.

Importantly, metamorphosis does not produce a "better version" of the old self. It produces a different orientation altogether. Leaders no longer rely on control to generate results. They no longer need to defend identity. They operate from essence rather than image and are therefore free to respond.

This shift is irreversible. Once a leader has reorganized at this level, returning to purely ego-driven leadership feels constricting rather than safe. What once felt powerful now feels limiting.

Metamorphosis marks the transition from managing complexity to inhabiting it. From leading through authority to leading through presence. From exerting power to allowing power to flow through alignment.

This is the point at which transformation becomes visible, embodied in a different quality of leadership that others can sense and trust.

When David became CEO, clarity was his signature. He was known for synthesizing information quickly, drawing sharp conclusions, and making decisive calls that drove execution with precision. In environments where speed, clarity, and control were rewarded, these qualities made him highly effective.

Investors trusted him. His team relied on him. When things became ambiguous, David stepped in and resolved them. For years, this worked exceptionally well.

As the company grew, however, something subtle began to change. The organization became more complex—more voices, more interdependencies, more uncertainty. Decisions that once felt clean now produced unintended consequences. Teams executed quickly, but alignment frayed. Momentum remained high, yet trust quietly eroded.

David responded the way he always had: by sharpening direction. He clarified priorities, tightened decision rights, and increased oversight. From his perspective, the system needed more leadership, not less.

From the system's perspective, something else was happening. The more David imposed certainty, the more people deferred rather than engaged. Meetings became quieter. Conversations moved into side channels. Initiative slowed—not from lack of effort, but from hesitation. People waited to be told what mattered, even as David asked for ownership.

Performance metrics still looked acceptable. On paper, the company was fine. If anything had shifted beneath the surface, it hadn't yet registered as a problem—only as a background tension he ignored.

The moment of rupture came during a strategy offsite. After hours of debate, David laid out what he believed was a clear and compelling path forward. He expected relief. Instead, the room went silent.

Finally, one of his senior leaders spoke. Carefully. Respectfully.

"I think we're waiting for you to tell us the answer," she said. "And I don't think you have it yet. I don't think any of us do."

David felt the familiar surge of irritation rise. His instinct was to reassert control, to explain, and to refine the logic. But something stopped him. Not insight, but exhaustion. The kind that comes from carrying the responsibility of having the answers for too long, from holding certainty together even as the system grows more complex.

For the first time, he noticed how much effort it was taking just to stay in control.

He didn't respond immediately. The silence stretched. Uncomfortable. Exposed.

"I don't know," he said finally. And then, after a pause, "I don't know what the next answer is."

The admission felt like a small death.

In the weeks that followed, David resisted the urge to replace uncertainty with action. He showed up differently. He listened more than he spoke. When asked for decisions, he slowed the conversation rather than closing it. This did not feel like leadership to him. It felt like letting go of the very thing that had once made him effective.

Internally, he wrestled with fear. If he wasn't the one providing clarity, who was he? What was his value? What if the organization drifted?

Externally, something unexpected began to happen. People spoke more freely. Tension surfaced through honest disagreement, unspoken concerns brought into the open, and assumptions tested in real time. The system began to reveal itself.

David noticed that his role was shifting. He was no longer directing movement but sensing it. He wasn't driving outcomes but creating conditions. The need to protect his identity as "the decisive leader" softened. In its place came a quieter orientation—attention, curiosity, and presence.

Over time, decisions began to arise organically—more coherently and with greater shared ownership. Authority redistributed. David's influence deepened as his need for control diminished.

What had dissolved was not his authority, but his attachment to being the source of it.

Looking back, David would not describe the experience as a breakthrough. It felt more like a shedding. The loss of something that had once been necessary, but no longer was.

"I didn't become less of a leader," he later reflected. "I became less attached to my authority. And everything changed."

The organization didn't transform overnight. But it stabilized in a new way. Less dependent. More resilient. More alive.

David learned to lead from presence rather than performance, allowing leadership to flow through him rather than be driven by him.

## New Operating Principles

After transformation, leadership does not return to business as usual. It operates from a different set of principles—not adopted but discovered through experience.

These principles are not rules or techniques. They are the natural consequences of a leader who no longer relies on ego, certainty, or control as primary sources of authority.

One of the most visible shifts is a movement from control to coherence. Instead of attempting to manage every variable, leaders focus on aligning purpose, values, and action. When coherence is present, less force is required. Systems begin to self-correct, and people move with greater clarity and ownership.

Authority also changes form. Rather than being asserted through position or expertise, it is communicated through the leader's steadiness, self-regulation, and coherence. Leaders speak less, but their words carry more weight. Decisions feel grounded rather than imposed. Influence arises from trust rather than control.

Problem-solving deepens into seeing patterns beneath the

surface. Rather than reacting to symptoms, leaders see them as signals and look deeper. They ask better questions, tolerate ambiguity, and resist premature conclusions. Over time, they address root dynamics instead of surface effects.

Certainty is replaced by grounded direction. Leaders no longer require full predictability in order to move forward. They act from clear principles and values, adjusting course as reality unfolds rather than forcing outcomes to match fixed plans. This allows them to remain responsive without becoming reactive, and adaptive without losing integrity.

Action itself becomes different. It arises from clarity rather than compulsion. It is guided by attunement to the moment rather than pressure. Leaders learn when to move decisively and when to wait. Both are conscious expressions of leadership.

Accountability deepens. Expectations become shared agreements, upheld with clarity and integrity. Responsibility is trusted and, when it falters, it is addressed directly and cleanly.

Perhaps the most profound shift is in how leaders relate to time horizons. Decisions are no longer evaluated solely for their immediate results but for their effects on people, culture, and the conditions they create for the future. Short-term gains that compromise long-term vitality lose their appeal.

These operating principles are quieter than traditional models of leadership, but more powerful. They do not rely on constant effort or force. They emerge naturally when leaders have crossed the threshold of transformation and no longer need to protect who they are.

Leadership, at this stage, moves beyond managing complexity and becomes the capacity to inhabit it with clarity, steadiness, and care.

## Expanded Consciousness

As transformation stabilizes, leaders do not simply operate differently; they perceive differently. Expanded consciousness is not an altered state or peak experience. It is an expanded range of awareness. Leaders can see more, hold more, and respond with greater creativity than before.

One of the most significant shifts is the ability to perceive wholes rather than isolated events. Leaders begin to recognize patterns beneath surface behavior; how incentives quietly shape decisions, how fear propagates through systems, and how unspoken assumptions influence outcomes.[17] This systems-level perception reduces reactivity and replaces it with discernment.

Expanded consciousness also brings a greater capacity to hold paradox. Leaders no longer feel compelled to resolve tension prematurely. They can hold urgency and care, accountability and compassion, structure and flexibility without collapsing into either/or thinking. This capacity allows solutions to emerge that are both creative and durable.

With broader awareness comes a different quality of power. Not louder or more forceful, but steadier. Influence replaces pressure. Clarity replaces persuasion. Leaders no longer rely on convincing others; coherence does the work. Their presence becomes stabilizing, especially in moments of uncertainty.

Another capacity that emerges is a refined relationship to intuition. Intuition matures into integrated knowing—insight informed by experience, refined pattern recognition, and deep listening. Analysis remains essential, but it now participates in a wider field of awareness. Decisions arise with inner clarity, not just mental certainty.

Expanded consciousness also transforms how leaders relate to time. They are no longer driven by reactive urgency. Instead, they discern what truly requires immediate action and what calls for patience. This temporal sensitivity allows them to intervene less frequently, yet with greater impact.

Perhaps most importantly, expanded consciousness opens access to new possibilities. When identity and certainty loosen, imagination expands. Leaders are no longer confined to futures that are extensions of the past. Innovation shifts from chasing novelty to cultivating what is coherent and life-giving within the system.

These capacities emerge organically from inner transformation. As consciousness expands, leadership expands with it. Transformation, therefore, becomes foundational in an increasingly complex, interconnected, and rapidly evolving world.

## TAKEAWAYS

- Conscious transformation is a threshold crossing.

  It reorients how leaders perceive, decide, and act. It shifts identity at the source rather than optimizing behavior at the surface.

- Letting go initiates transformation.

  Leaders release what has completed its purpose—even when it once brought success, stability, or recognition.

- Death and rebirth are structural to real change.

  Old identities, roles, and protective strategies dissolve before new capacities can stabilize.

- The ego must loosen its dominance.

  What once provided safety and coherence cannot remain the primary center of leadership as complexity increases.

- The unknown is a generative space.

  Disciplined patience allows emergence to unfold without collapsing uncertainty into premature control.

- Metamorphosis reorganizes leadership from within.

  Action begins to arise from essence rather than image, and response replaces reaction.

- New operating principles naturally emerge.

  Coherence replaces control. Presence deepens authority. Sense-making precedes problem-solving. Agreements strengthen accountability.

- Expanded consciousness increases capacity.

  Leaders perceive systems more fully, hold paradox without fragmentation, and integrate intellect with intuition.

- Transformation scales through systems.

  Leadership patterns—conscious or unconscious—are amplified by culture, structure, and technology.

- Transformation is now a responsibility.

  In an era of accelerating complexity, leaders who do not evolve internally risk magnifying distortion at scale.

## PRACTICES

These practices support the deeper shifts of transformation—where familiar identities loosen and new ways of being begin to emerge.

They are not meant to be completed quickly or in sequence. Each one invites reflection, patience, and a willingness to stay present as something old releases and something new takes shape.

### 1. Letting Go Inventory

Transformation begins by recognizing what has reached its natural completion. This practice invites you to notice where energy is being used to sustain something that has already run its course.

Identify one role, identity, belief, or leadership habit that once served you well but now feels constraining. Resist the urge to immediately change it. Simply name it—and observe how much effort it requires to maintain.

*What am I still holding that has already fulfilled its purpose?*

### 2. Practicing Surrender Without Withdrawal

Surrender in leadership is not withdrawal. It is the release of control over outcomes that can no longer be engineered from your current way of being.

Choose one situation where you feel pressure to provide answers prematurely. Stay present without rushing resolution. Continue to engage, listen, and support the process—allowing clarity to emerge rather than forcing it into form.

*Where am I trying to force clarity instead of allowing emergence?*

**3. Staying with Not-Knowing**

The space between dissolution and renewal is uncomfortable—and generative. This practice strengthens your capacity to remain steady when certainty dissolves.

When anxiety arises from not knowing what comes next, notice the impulse to fill the gap. Name the uncertainty. Stay with it. Observe what becomes visible when you allow space rather than collapsing it.

*How do I respond to uncertainty—and what becomes possible when I stay with it?*

**4. Releasing Ego Protection**

Transformation loosens defensive patterns that once provided safety but now limit perception.

Notice moments when your leadership feels reactive, defensive, or overly invested in being right. Rather than correcting the behavior, explore the identity being protected.

*What identity am I defending—and what might open if I loosened my grip on it?*

**5. Leading from Essence**

As transformation stabilizes, leadership begins to arise from a deeper center.

Before making an important decision, pause and examine the source of your impulse. *Does it arise from fear, habit, image, or expectation—or from clarity and alignment?*

*From where is this decision emerging: image or essence?*

### 6. Sensing Transformation at Scale

Transformation extends beyond the individual. Leadership shapes systems, and systems amplify patterns.

Reflect on how you show up, where you place your attention, and the choices you make—and how they influence culture, pace, and trust. Notice which patterns are being reinforced through structure, technology, or policy.

*What is being amplified through my leadership right now?*

# Closing Remarks

Leadership has always been an act of creation. What has changed is the scale.

Never before have human choices been amplified so quickly or carried so far. Technologies, systems, and institutions now extend intention across time and distance in ways previous generations could not have imagined. What once remained local now becomes global. What once unfolded slowly now accelerates. What once could be corrected over time now hardens into structure and system.

In this environment, leadership is never neutral. Every decision shapes conditions. Every omission carries consequence. Every form of unconsciousness scales.

This is an invitation to awareness—not perfection.

Throughout this book, we have explored leadership not as control, authority, or performance, but as conscious creation—the capacity to shape reality with clarity, integrity, and care. We have examined what it means to lead from within, to lead with others, and to lead with impact. At every level, the invitation has been the same: to notice the source from which leadership arises.

Because the future is not shaped only by what we build, but by the consciousness from which we build it.

At its heart, conscious leadership is the conscious creation of beauty, strength, and love—in ourselves, in others, and out in the world. Beauty as coherence and wholeness. Strength as grounded capacity without domination. Love as care that honors dignity, life, and future generations. These qualities shape how systems function, how power is exercised, and how the future unfolds.

When leaders act from fear, fear is amplified. When leaders act from urgency without reflection, reactive urgency becomes embedded in systems. When leaders act from ego or unexamined certainty, those patterns harden into culture, policy, and technology.

And when leaders act from presence, coherence, and conscious choice, a different trajectory begins to take shape.

This is why conscious leadership is no longer a personal preference or a philosophical orientation. It is a practical responsibility. The question is no longer whether leaders have power, but whether they are aware of what that power is shaping.

The future will be created regardless. The only open question is how. Not by a single leader or institution, but through countless moments of choice—often quiet, often unseen—made each day in families, teams, organizations, communities, and systems around the world.

Each of us participates in this shaping. Leadership is not reserved for positions of authority; it is inherent in being human. Wherever we influence what is created—at home, at work, in a relationship—we are leading. No one stands outside the formation of the future. What we build, what we allow, and what we ignore all become part of it.

The accumulation of these moments determines whether the future we inherit is brittle or resilient, depleting or life-giving, fragmented or whole.

Conscious creation does not ask leaders to control the future. It invites them to participate in its unfolding with humility and care—cultivating the courage to release what no longer fits, the patience to remain present in uncertainty, the integrity to act from essence rather than image, and the willingness to recognize that what we amplify ultimately reflects who we are.

Nowhere is this responsibility more visible than in the systems that shape the next generation; foremost among them, education.

For much of modern history, education was organized around the efficient transfer of information. That made sense in a world where knowledge was scarce, and specialization was stable. That world no longer exists.

Today, information is abundant, searchable, and increasingly generated by machines. Artificial intelligence can analyze, generate, simulate, and optimize at extraordinary speed. What it does not supply is wisdom.

Meaningful lives and responsible leadership have never been shaped by information alone, but by awareness, discernment, creativity, ethical clarity, emotional intelligence, courage, and the capacity to navigate uncertainty. These qualities cannot be automated or outsourced. They must be cultivated.

Education, at its deepest level, is not about information. It is about formation.

It shapes how human beings perceive, relate, decide, and create, and therefore the consciousness that will guide the powerful tools now entering the world.

Approached consciously, education becomes a practice ground

for leadership itself, where people learn not only how to think, but how to choose, relate, and take responsibility for what they bring into being. Technology then becomes an amplifier of human wisdom rather than a substitute for it.

What we choose to cultivate here will shape far more than workforce readiness. It will shape the quality of leadership, the integrity of our systems, and the kind of future our tools ultimately serve.

If there is a final invitation in this book, it is this:

To lead not as a reaction to the world as it is, but as a conscious creator of the world that is emerging.

What we shape shapes us in return. What we create becomes the ground others will stand on.

The future is already being formed. The work now is to choose—again and again—from a deeper place, and to create consciously what others will one day inherit.

# References

## Part I: Leading From Within

1. Norman Doidge, *The Brain That Changes Itself: Stories of Personal Triumph from the Frontiers of Brain Science* (New York: Penguin Life, 2007).

2. Elaine Hatfield, John T. Cacioppo, and Richard L. Rapson, *Emotional Contagion* (Cambridge: Cambridge University Press, 1994).

3. Sylvain Laborde, Emma Mosley, and Julian F. Thayer, "Heart Rate Variability and Cardiac Vagal Tone in Psychophysiological Research—Recommendations for Experiment Planning, Data Analysis, and Data Reporting," *Frontiers in Psychology* 8 (2017): 213, https://doi.org/10.3389/fpsyg.2017.00213.

4. Patricia Jerath et al., "Physiology of Long Pranayamic Breathing," *Medical Hypotheses* 67, no. 3 (2006): 566–571.

5. Stephen W. Porges, *The Polyvagal Theory: Neurophysiological Foundations of Emotions, Attachment, Communication, and Self-Regulation* (New York: Norton, 2011).

6. Julian F. Thayer and Richard D. Lane, "A Model of Neurovisceral Integration in Emotion Regulation," *Journal of Affective Disorders* 61 (2000): 201–216.

7. David Spiegel et al., "Brief Structured Respiration Practices Enhance Mood and Reduce Physiological Arousal," *Cell Reports Medicine* 4, no. 1 (2023).

8. Marcus E. Raichle et al., "A Default Mode of Brain Function," *Proceedings of the National Academy of Sciences* 98, no. 2 (2001): 676–682.

9. Stephen W. Porges, *The Polyvagal Theory: Neurophysiological Foundations of Emotions, Attachment, Communication, and Self-Regulation* (New York: W. W. Norton, 2011).

10. Lawrence W. Barsalou, "Grounded Cognition," *Annual Review of Psychology* 59 (2008): 617–645.

11. Amy F. T. Arnsten, "Stress Signalling Pathways That Impair Prefrontal Cortex Structure and Function," *Nature Reviews Neuroscience* 10, no. 6 (2009): 410–422.

12. Michael Merzenich, *Soft-Wired: How the New Science of Brain Plasticity Can Change Your Life* (San Francisco: Parnassus Publishing, 2013).

13. Stephen W. Porges, *The Polyvagal Theory: Neurophysiological Foundations of Emotions, Attachment, Communication, and Self-Regulation* (New York: W. W. Norton, 2011).

14. Erik Brynjolfsson and Andrew McAfee, *The Second Machine Age: Work, Progress, and Prosperity in a Time of Brilliant Technologies* (New York: W. W. Norton, 2014).

15. Stanislav Grof, *The Adventure of Self-Discovery: Dimensions of Consciousness and New Perspectives in Psychotherapy and Inner Exploration* (Albany: State University of New York Press, 1988).

16. Roland R. Griffiths et al., "Psilocybin Produces Substantial and Sustained Decreases in Depression and Anxiety in Patients with Life-Threatening Cancer," *Journal of Psychopharmacology* 30, no. 12 (2016): 1181–1197.

17. Richard C. Schwartz, *Internal Family Systems Therapy*, 2nd ed. (New York: Guilford Press, 2019).

18. George Pransky, *The Relationship Handbook: How to Understand and Improve Every Relationship in Your Life* (New York: Prentice Hall Press, 2006).

## Part II: Leading With Others

1. Stanislas Dehaene, *Consciousness and the Brain: Deciphering How the Brain Codes Our Thoughts* (New York: Viking, 2014).

2. Andy Clark, *Surfing Uncertainty: Prediction, Action, and the Embodied Mind* (Oxford: Oxford University Press, 2016).

3. Joseph E. LeDoux, *The Emotional Brain: The Mysterious Underpinnings of Emotional Life* (New York: Simon & Schuster, 1996).

4. Carl R. Rogers, *On Becoming a Person: A Therapist's View of Psychotherapy* (Boston: Houghton Mifflin, 1961).

5. Lisa Feldman Barrett, *How Emotions Are Made: The Secret Life of the Brain* (Boston: Houghton Mifflin Harcourt, 2017).

6. Daniel J. Siegel, *The Developing Mind: How Relationships and the Brain Interact to Shape Who We Are*, 2nd ed. (New York: Guilford Press, 2012).

7. Stephen W. Porges, *The Polyvagal Theory: Neurophysiological Foundations of Emotions, Attachment, Communication, and Self-Regulation* (New York: W. W. Norton, 2011).

8. Denise M. Rousseau, *Psychological Contracts in Organizations: Understanding Written and Unwritten Agreements* (Thousand Oaks, CA: SAGE, 1995).

9. Amy C. Edmondson, *The Fearless Organization: Creating Psychological Safety in the Workplace for Learning, Innovation, and Growth* (Hoboken, NJ: Wiley, 2018).

10. Daniel J. Siegel, *The Developing Mind: How Relationships and the Brain Interact to Shape Who We Are*, 2nd ed. (New York: Guilford Press, 2012).

11. Stephen W. Porges, *The Polyvagal Theory: Neurophysiological Foundations of Emotions, Attachment, Communication, and Self-Regulation* (New York: W. W. Norton, 2011).

12. Peter Senge et al., *Presence: Human Purpose and the Field of the Future* (New York: Doubleday, 2004).

## Part III: Leading With Impact

1. Richard J. Davidson and Sharon Begley, *The Emotional Life of Your Brain* (New York: Hudson Street Press, 2012).

2. Daniel J. Siegel, *The Mindful Brain: Reflection and Attunement in the Cultivation of Well-Being* (New York: W. W. Norton, 2007).

3. Emeran Mayer, *The Mind-Gut Connection: How the Hidden Conversation Within Our Bodies Impacts Our Mood, Our Choices, and Our Overall Health* (New York: Harper Wave, 2016).

4. Sigal G. Barsade, "The Ripple Effect: Emotional Contagion and Its Influence on Group Behavior," *Administrative Science Quarterly* 47, no. 4 (2002): 644–675.

5. Mihaly Csikszentmihalyi, *Flow: The Psychology of Optimal Experience* (New York: Harper & Row, 1990).

6. Sigal G. Barsade, "The Ripple Effect: Emotional Contagion and Its Influence on Group Behavior," *Administrative Science Quarterly* 47, no. 4 (2002): 644–675.

7. Otto Scharmer, *Theory U: Leading from the Future as It Emerges*, 2nd ed. (San Francisco: Berrett-Koehler, 2016).

8. Peter M. Senge, *The Fifth Discipline: The Art and Practice of the Learning Organization* (New York: Doubleday, 2006).

9. Bessel van der Kolk, *The Body Keeps the Score: Brain, Mind, and Body in the Healing of Trauma* (New York: Viking, 2014).

10. Stephen W. Porges, *The Polyvagal Theory: Neurophysiological Foundations of Emotions, Attachment, Communication, and Self-Regulation* (New York: W. W. Norton, 2011).

11. Edward L. Deci and Richard M. Ryan, *Self-Determination Theory: Basic Psychological Needs in Motivation, Development, and Wellness* (New York: Guilford Press, 2017).

12. Amy C. Edmondson, *The Fearless Organization: Creating Psychological Safety in the Workplace for Learning, Innovation, and Growth* (Hoboken, NJ: Wiley, 2019).

13. National Institute of Standards and Technology, *Artificial Intelligence Risk Management Framework (AI RMF 1.0)* (Gaithersburg, MD: NIST, 2023).

14. Robert Kegan, *In Over Our Heads: The Mental Demands of Modern Life* (Cambridge, MA: Harvard University Press, 1994).

15. William Bridges, *Transitions: Making Sense of Life's Changes*, 2nd ed. (Cambridge, MA: Da Capo Press, 2004).

16. Ronald A. Heifetz, *Leadership Without Easy Answers* (Cambridge, MA: Harvard University Press, 1994).

17. Donella H. Meadows, *Thinking in Systems: A Primer*, ed. Diana Wright (White River Junction, VT: Chelsea Green Publishing, 2008).

# Acknowledgements

This book is the result of many conversations, experiences, and moments of reflection over the years. While my name appears on the cover, the ideas within it have been shaped through the people I have had the privilege to learn from, work with, and walk alongside.

I am grateful to my family for the space, patience, and perspective that made this work possible.

To the leaders and clients I have had the privilege to work with over the years—thank you for your openness, your trust, and your courage to engage in deeper conversations. Much of what is written here has been refined through our shared exploration of what it means to lead with awareness and intention.

I am especially grateful to the early readers of this manuscript—Zohre Elahian, Brad Mountz, Justin Wang, and Kiran Rapal—for their thoughtful reflections and willingness to engage with these ideas as they were still taking shape. Your insights helped bring greater clarity and depth to this work.

I am also grateful to the teachers, thinkers, and traditions that have shaped my understanding of consciousness, leadership, and human potential. Their influence is woven throughout this work.

This book is part of an ongoing journey—one that continues to unfold.

# About the Author

Nader Vasseghi is an executive coach, author, entrepreneur, and musician whose work focuses on conscious leadership and the expansion of human potential. He advises founders, CEOs, and senior executives, helping them navigate complexity, lead with greater clarity, and build organizations that create lasting value.

Drawing on decades of experience across business, psychology, systems thinking, and contemplative practice, Nader is known for helping leaders move beyond reactive habits and inherited models of authority toward a more conscious and generative form of leadership. His work integrates inner mastery with practical execution, supporting leaders in developing the awareness, resilience, and relational intelligence required in an era of accelerating change.

Nader is the author of *Path to Freedom: Leading a Life of Joy, Impact, and Abundance.* His work centers on a simple yet powerful idea: leadership is an act of conscious creation—the capacity to shape conditions in which beauty, strength, and love can emerge in ourselves, in others, and in the world.

He leads immersive leadership retreats at the Center for Conscious Creation in Carmel, California, where leaders step away from the pressures of daily life to engage in deeper reflection, renewal, and transformation.

In addition to his work with executives, Nader is a musician and composer. Through sound and music, he explores the same principles that guide his leadership philosophy—presence, listening, creativity, and the emergence of authentic expression.

Across all of his work, Nader's aim is to support leaders in shaping the future from a deeper level of awareness and responsibility. Leaders who resonate with this work often reach out to explore deeper collaboration through coaching or retreat experiences.

# A GIFT FOR YOU

If the ideas in this book resonate with you, I would like to offer you a complimentary resource that may support you in applying these principles in your own leadership.

### 10 Practices of Conscious Leadership

This practical resource expands on the principles explored in this book and offers simple yet powerful practices to help you:

- Develop greater clarity and presence as a leader
- Navigate complexity with calm and awareness
- Make more conscious and intentional decisions
- Cultivate deeper connection with your team

You can download the guide at:
**www.cnergist.com**

Visit the Assessments page to also explore the Conscious Leadership Assessment, a complimentary tool to discover where you currently stand across the three dimensions of conscious leadership — Leading From Within, Leading With Others, and Leading With Impact.

My hope is that these practices support you in bringing more awareness, intention, and creativity into your leadership and your life.

—Nader Vasseghi

Made in the USA
Coppell, TX
01 August 2026

85446562R00157